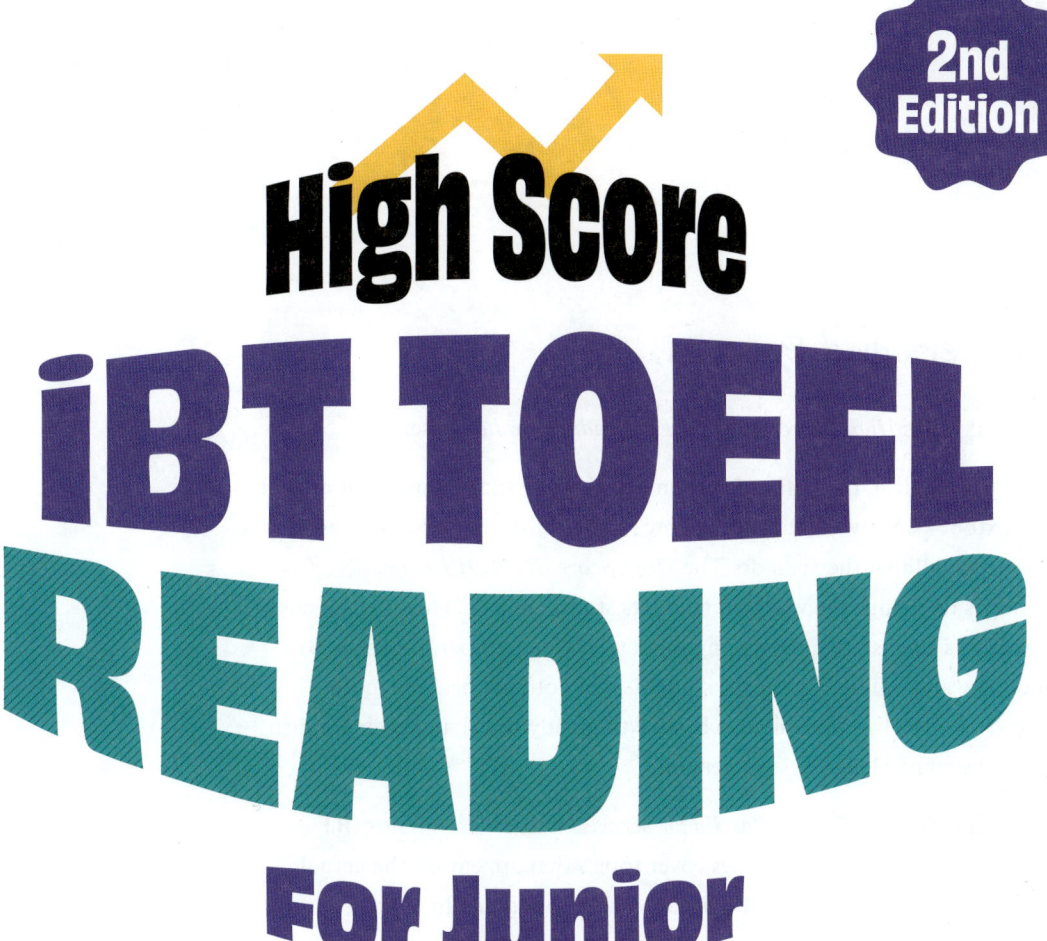

Dear Teachers and Parents,

Welcome to Darakwon's *High Score iBT TOEFL Reading for Junior* series.

When people study English, they often focus on learning the same topics that appear in all English textbooks. So while they learn how to have basic conversations with people, that is about all that they can do. The *High Score iBT TOEFL Reading for Junior series* hopes to change the way that students study English. This series focuses on teaching students English by introducing them to a wide number of topics. By learning about new and different subjects, students will not only become more interested in learning English but will also be able to greatly to expand their English vocabulary and their knowledge base in general.

The *High Score iBT TOEFL Reading for Junior* series is written as a junior iBT TOEFL textbook. The books in this series cover topics that appear on the actual iBT TOEFL test. The questions in the books are also phrased just like those that students will find on the iBT TOEFL test. This should help familiarize students with the iBT TOEFL test and prepare them for when they take it in the future. By learning as much as they can about the iBT TOEFL test prior to taking it, the students will ensure that they will have some knowledge of many of the topics on the test and will be comfortable with the style of the test and the questions on it. All of these factors should lead to higher scores for the students.

It is my hope that students will use this series first to improve their knowledge of English. They will find the passages have been written at a level that they will be able to understand, and the students should find the passages themselves to be fun to read and full of interesting facts and information. Or course, as a junior iBT TOEFL book, a major emphasis of the series is to familiarize the students with the iBT TOEFL test. Most of all, I hope that this series will instill a love of English in students and inspire them to continue and to advance their studies of the English language.

Michael A. Putlack

Table of CONTENTS

About the TOEFL 4

How to Use This Book 8

Chapter 1 History (Chronological Order) 13

Chapter 2 Geography (Comparison and Contrast) 31

Chapter 3 Technology (Cause and Effect) 49

Chapter 4 Education (Classification) 67

Chapter 5 Economics (Guessing Unknown Words) 85

Chapter 6 Sociology (Mapping) 103

Chapter 7 Exploration (Identifying Cohesive Devices) 121

Chapter 8 Environment (Outlining) 139

Actual Test 157

About the TOEFL

The TOEFL iBT

TOEFL is the Test of English as a Foreign Language. It measures the test taker's ability in English. Foreign students often need to take the TOEFL to get into an American college or university. For that reason, the TOEFL exam is very important.

The TOEFL iBT is an Internet-based test (iBT). Students take the TOEFL iBT on a computer at one of the test centers.

The TOEFL iBT tests four language skills. These skills are reading, listening, speaking, and writing. There are many different kinds of passages, lectures, conversations, and questions. Many sections combine two or more of these skills. So students must be capable in several English skills to get high scores on the exam.

The Format of the TOEFL iBT

There are four sections on the TOEFL iBT. These sections are Reading, Listening, Speaking, and Writing.

The Reading section has two passages. These passages are around 700 words long with 10 questions per passage. The Reading section of the test takes 35 minutes.

The Listening section has two types of passages. They are lectures and conversations. Each Listening section has 3 lectures. The lectures are 3-5 minutes each with 6 questions per lecture. Each listening section has 2 conversations. The conversations are 3 minutes each with 5 questions per conversation. The Listening section of the test takes 36 minutes.

The Speaking section has two types of questions. They are independent and integrated questions. There is 1 independent question. The independent question asks about your own ideas, opinions, and experiences. There are 3 integrated questions. The integrated questions consist of conversations, reading passages, lectures, or combinations of them—just as you would see in or out of a classroom. They ask questions based on the reading and listening passages. The Speaking section of the test takes 16 minutes.

The Writing section has two types of questions: 1 integrated task and 1 academic discussion task. The integrated task combines a short reading passage and a short lecture. The test taker must then write an essay about these two. The academic discussion task asks a question about a personal experience or opinion. The test taker must then write an essay about this question. The Writing section of the test takes 29 minutes.

The New Test Format

Test Section	Number of Questions	Timing	Score
Reading	• 2 passages, 10 questions each	35 minutes	30
Listening	• 3 lectures, 6 questions each • 2 conversations, 5 questions each	36 minutes	30
Speaking	• 1 independent task • 3 integrated tasks	16 minutes	30
Writing	• 1 integrated task • 1 academic discussion task	29 minutes	30

The Reading Section

There are 10 different kinds of questions in the Reading section. Each question appears a different number of times.

The different kinds of questions are:

1. **Factual Information Questions**
   These ask about the facts in the passage.
   There are 1-3 of these questions in each passage.

2. **Negative Factual Questions**
   These ask about information that is NOT in the passage or which is NOT true.
   There are 0-2 of these questions in each passage.

3. **Inference Questions**
   These ask about information the test taker must infer from the passage.
   There are 0-2 of these questions in each passage.

4. **Rhetorical Purpose Questions**
   These ask about the reason why the author includes some information in the passage.
   There are 0-2 of these questions in each passage.

5. **Vocabulary Questions**
   These ask about the definitions of words or phrases in the passage.
   There are 1-3 of these questions in each passage.

6. **Reference Questions**
   These ask which word or words another word in the passage refers to.
   There are 0-1 of these questions in each passage.

About the TOEFL

7 Sentence Simplification Questions
These take one long sentence from the passage and ask the test taker to find a simplified version of that sentence. There are 0-1 of these questions in each passage.

8 Insert Text Questions
These show the test taker a new sentence and ask the test taker to determine where the sentence would fit best in the passage. There are 0-1 of these questions in each passage.

9 Prose Summary Questions
These provide a summary of the passage and then ask the test taker to choose 3 of 6 sentences that best relate to the summary. There are 0-1 of these questions in each passage.

10 Fill in a Table Questions
These ask the test taker to categorize various facts and information that appear in the passage. There are 0-1 of these questions in each passage.

How to Use This Book

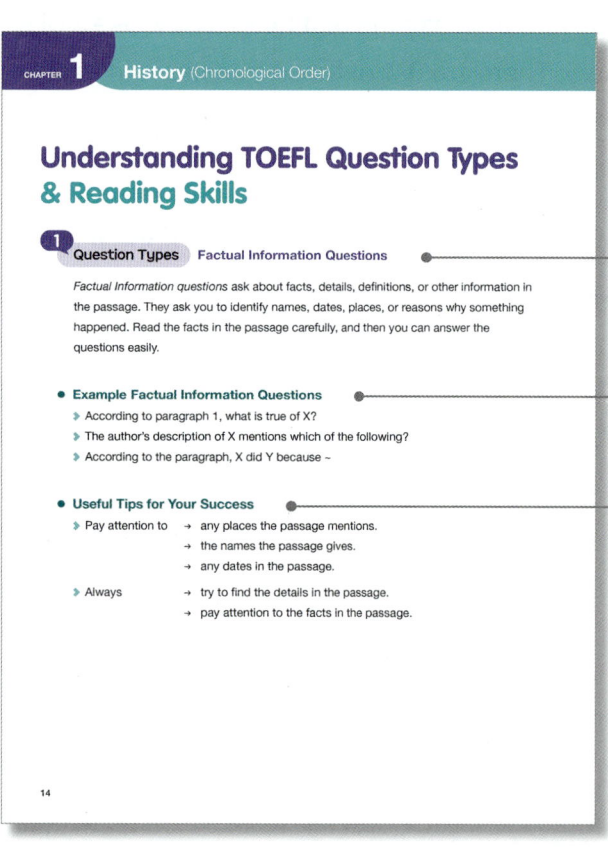

Question Types
This section describes the question or questions covered in the chapter. It provides an explanation of each question and how to try to answer it.

Example Questions
This section shows the different ways that the questions appear on the TOEFL test. Students can learn how to recognize the different types of question in this section.

Useful Tips for Your Success
This section provides various tips on how to answer questions properly. It also provides hints on right and wrong approaches to answering each question.

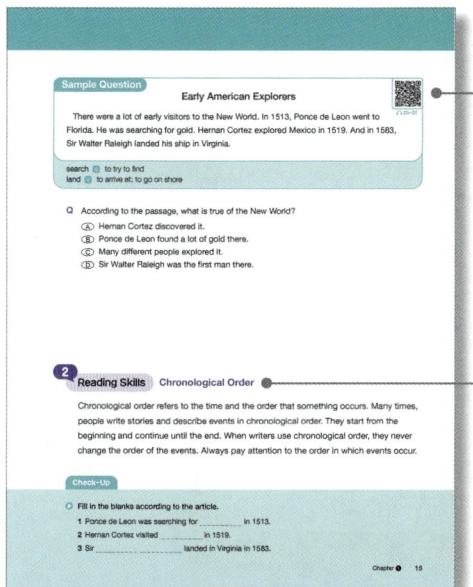

Sample Question
This is a short 40-word passage on one of the topics in the unit. It has one TOEFL question and one reading skills question.

Reading Skills
This is an explanation of the reading skill that the chapter covers.

Exercises

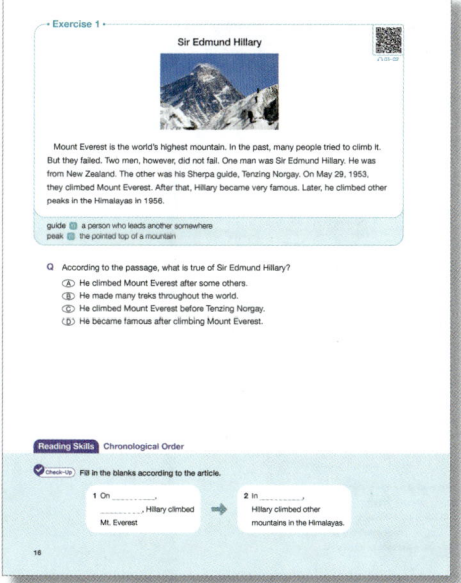

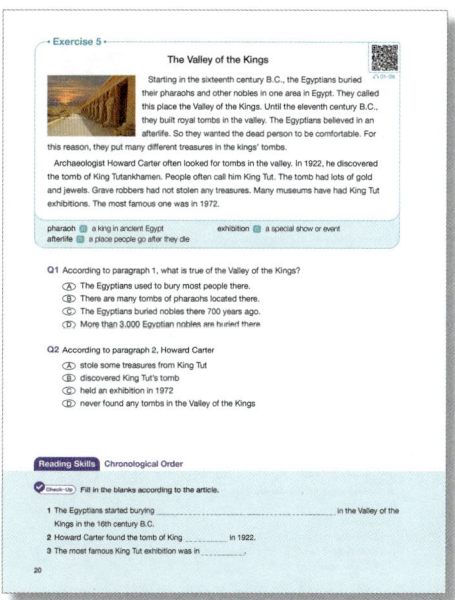

Short Passages
There are four short passages with 40-60 words each. Each passage is on a topic that concerns the subject of the unit and has one TOEFL question and one reading skills question.

Medium Passages
There are four medium-length passages with 80-120 words each. Each passage is on a topic that concerns the subject of the unit and has two TOEFL questions and one reading skills question.

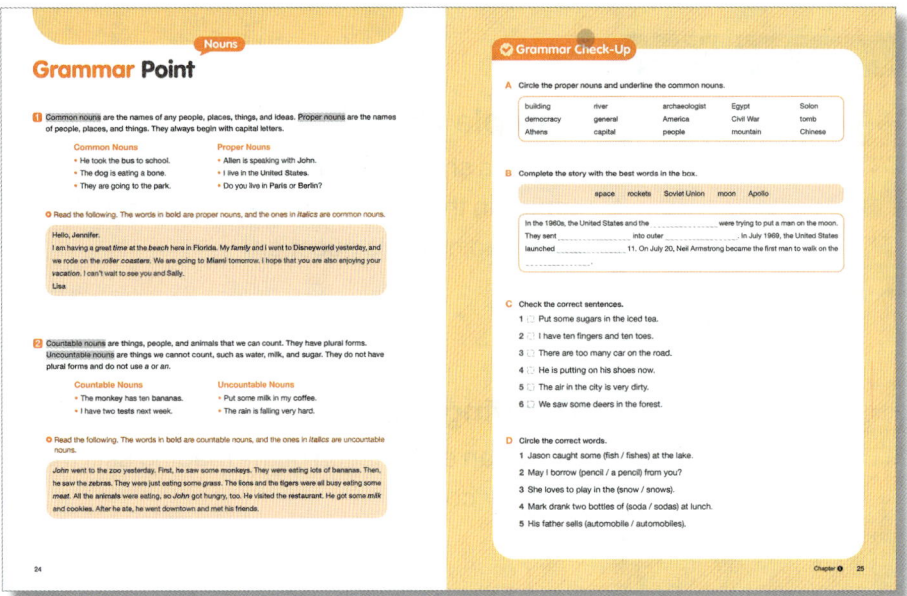

Grammar Point

This section explains a certain part of speech. It has one page of explanations and one page of various exercises for students to answer.

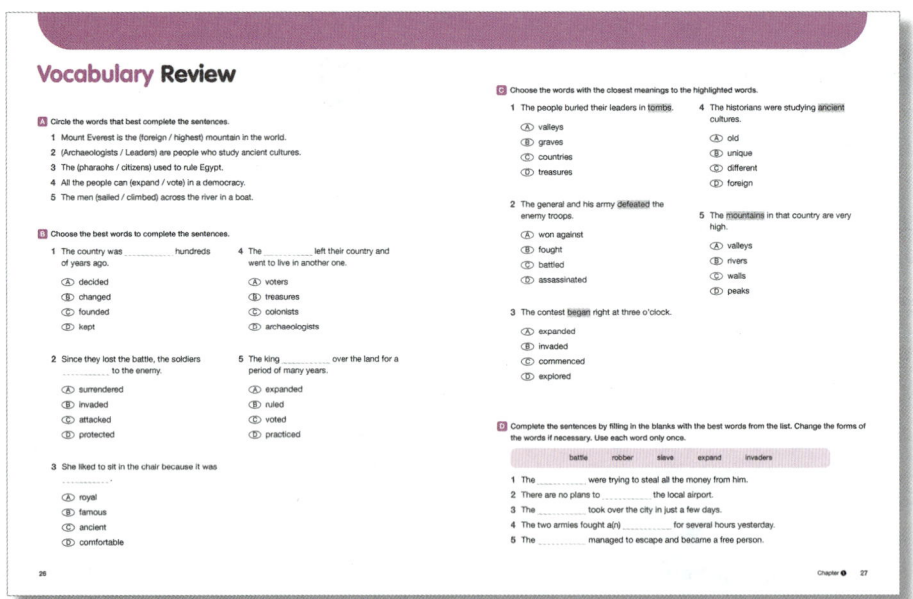

Vocabulary Review

This section provides a comprehensive review of the vocabulary found in the various passages in the unit. Each unit has twenty vocabulary review questions, and all of the answer choices are words that appear in the passages in the unit.

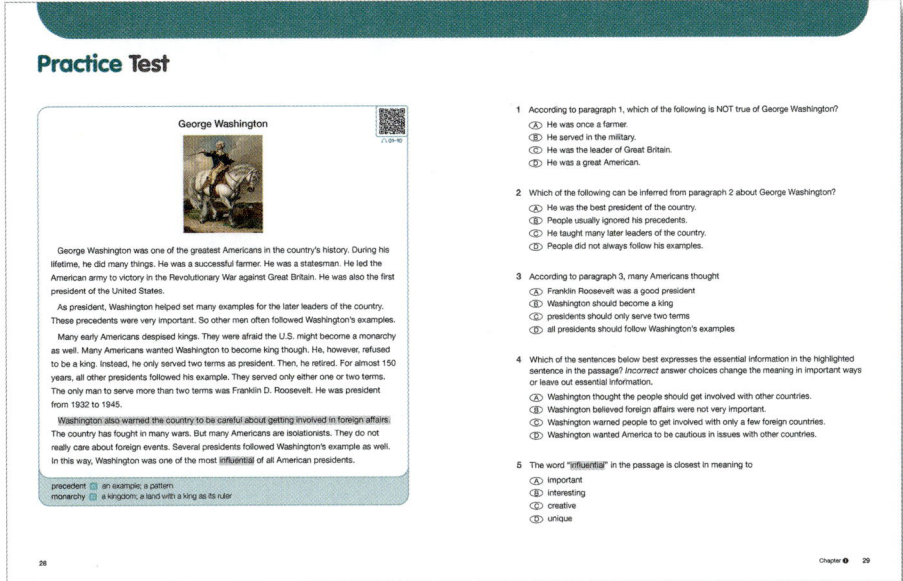

Practice Test

There is one passage with 120-180 words. The passage is on a topic that concerns the subject of the unit and has six TOEFL questions.

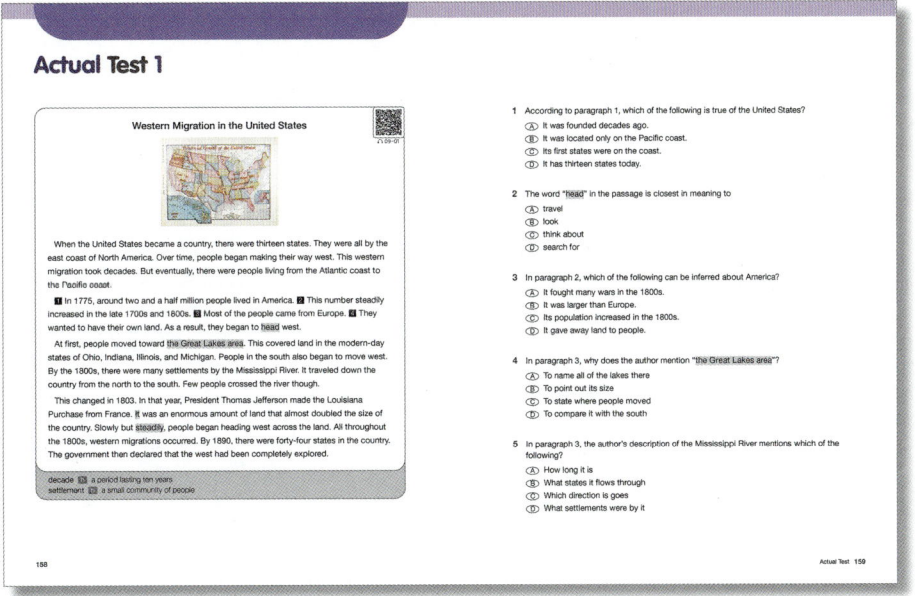

Actual Test

This section includes 3 passages with 180-220 words with 10 questions each. Every passage has different kinds of questions. There are questions from all 10 types found in the Reading section. Additionally, all of the passages are from topics that appear in the book. These passages and questions are shorter versions of a typical TOEFL iBT Reading section.

CHAPTER

01

History
(Chronological order)

1. Sir Edmund Hillary
2. The Great Wall of China
3. The Civil War
4. Julius Caesar
5. The Valley of the Kings
6. Washington Crosses the Delaware
7. Athenian Democracy
8. The Byzantine Empire

CHAPTER 1 History (Chronological Order)

Understanding TOEFL Question Types & Reading Skills

1 Question Types — Factual Information Questions

Factual Information questions ask about facts, details, definitions, or other information in the passage. They ask you to identify names, dates, places, or reasons why something happened. Read the facts in the passage carefully, and then you can answer the questions easily.

- **Example Factual Information Questions**
  - According to paragraph 1, what is true of X?
  - The author's description of X mentions which of the following?
  - According to the paragraph, X did Y because ~

- **Useful Tips for Your Success**
  - Pay attention to → any places the passage mentions.
    - → the names the passage gives.
    - → any dates in the passage.
  - Always → try to find the details in the passage.
    - → pay attention to the facts in the passage.

Sample Question

Early American Explorers

There were a lot of early visitors to the New World. In 1513, Ponce de Leon went to Florida. He was searching for gold. Hernan Cortez explored Mexico in 1519. And in 1583, Sir Walter Raleigh landed his ship in Virginia.

search v to try to find
land v to arrive at; to go on shore

Q According to the passage, what is true of the New World?
- Ⓐ Hernan Cortez discovered it.
- Ⓑ Ponce de Leon found a lot of gold there.
- Ⓒ Many different people explored it.
- Ⓓ Sir Walter Raleigh was the first man there.

2 Reading Skills — Chronological Order

Chronological order refers to the time and the order that something occurs. Many times, people write stories and describe events in chronological order. They start from the beginning and continue until the end. When writers use chronological order, they never change the order of the events. Always pay attention to the order in which events occur.

Check-Up

▶ Fill in the blanks according to the article.

1. Ponce de Leon was searching for _____ in 1513.
2. Hernan Cortez visited _____ in 1519.
3. Sir _____ _____ landed in Virginia in 1583.

• Exercise 1 •

Sir Edmund Hillary

 01-02

Mount Everest is the world's highest mountain. In the past, many people tried to climb it. But they failed. Two men, however, did not fail. One man was Sir Edmund Hillary. He was from New Zealand. The other was his Sherpa guide, Tenzing Norgay. On May 29, 1953, they climbed Mount Everest. After that, Hillary became very famous. Later, he climbed other peaks in the Himalayas in 1956.

guide n a person who leads another somewhere
peak n the pointed top of a mountain

Q According to the passage, what is true of Sir Edmund Hillary?
   Ⓐ He climbed Mount Everest after some others.
   Ⓑ He made many treks throughout the world.
   Ⓒ He climbed Mount Everest before Tenzing Norgay.
   Ⓓ He became famous after climbing Mount Everest.

Reading Skills Chronological Order

 Fill in the blanks according to the article.

1 On _____, _____, Hillary climbed Mt. Everest.

2 In _____, Hillary climbed other mountains in the Himalayas.

• **Exercise 2** •

The Great Wall of China

01-03

The Chinese Empire had many enemies. They often invaded China and attacked the people there. So the Chinese built a long wall. They started it around 400 B.C. They finished in the sixteenth century. They called it the Great Wall of China. The wall covers almost 4,000 miles. The Chinese put soldiers on the wall. They protected China against foreign invaders.

invade v to attack inside another person's country or area
foreign adj from a different country

Q According to the passage, the Chinese built the Great Wall of China because

Ⓐ they wanted to attack other countries from the wall
Ⓑ they needed a place to put all of their soldiers
Ⓒ they were protecting their land from their enemies
Ⓓ they used the wall to help them invade other countries

Reading Skills | Chronological Order

Check-Up Fill in the blanks according to the article.

| Invaders attacked the Chinese. | | 1 The Chinese started building the Great Wall in _____. | | 2 They finished the wall in the _____ century. | | Soldiers protected China with the wall. |

• **Exercise 3** •

The Civil War

In the nineteenth century, America had many problems. The North and the South were very different. Many Southerners owned slaves. But most Northerners did not. The North had factories. The South was mostly farms. Later, the two regions had many disagreements. They could not solve their problems. Finally, fighting commenced on April 12, 1861. The North later won the Civil War in 1865.

disagreement n an argument
commence v to begin

Q According to the passage, the Civil War occurred because

Ⓐ the North and the South could not solve their problems
Ⓑ the South did not have many factories
Ⓒ the North wanted to own more slaves
Ⓓ Northerners did not want to become farmers

Reading Skills **Chronological Order**

 Fill in the blanks according to the article.

1 The Civil War began on _____, _____.

2 The Civil War ended in _____.

• **Exercise 4** •

Julius Caesar

Julius Caesar was a great Roman general. He was born around 100 B.C. Later, he conquered Gaul with his army. Then, he became the dictator of Rome. Caesar made many reforms. He changed Roman social and political life. But many Romans hated him. So some senators assassinated him in 44 B.C. Sadly, Caesar could not make all of his changes.

conquer v to defeat in war
assassinate v to kill someone important

Q The author's description of Julius Caesar mentions which of the following?

Ⓐ How he completed his reforms
Ⓑ Why he assassinated a senator
Ⓒ When he conquered Gaul
Ⓓ How he served Rome

Reading Skills **Chronological Order**

Check-Up Insert a number from 1 to 4 in the correct order according to the article.

_____ Some senators killed him in 44 B.C.
_____ He and his army conquered Gaul.
_____ He became the dictator of Rome.
_____ Julius Caesar was born around 100 B.C.

• **Exercise 5** •

The Valley of the Kings

🎧 01-06

Starting in the sixteenth century B.C., the Egyptians buried their pharaohs and other nobles in one area in Egypt. They called this place the Valley of the Kings. Until the eleventh century B.C., they built royal tombs in the valley. The Egyptians believed in an afterlife. So they wanted the dead person to be comfortable. For this reason, they put many different treasures in the kings' tombs.

Archaeologist Howard Carter often looked for tombs in the valley. In 1922, he discovered the tomb of King Tutankhamen. People often call him King Tut. The tomb had lots of gold and jewels. Grave robbers had not stolen any treasures. Many museums have had King Tut exhibitions. The most famous one was in 1972.

pharaoh [n] a king in ancient Egypt
exhibition [n] a special show or event
afterlife [n] a place people go after they die

Q1 According to paragraph 1, what is true of the Valley of the Kings?

Ⓐ The Egyptians used to bury most people there.
Ⓑ There are many tombs of pharaohs located there.
Ⓒ The Egyptians buried nobles there 700 years ago.
Ⓓ More than 3,000 Egyptian nobles are buried there.

Q2 According to paragraph 2, Howard Carter

Ⓐ stole some treasures from King Tut
Ⓑ discovered King Tut's tomb
Ⓒ held an exhibition in 1972
Ⓓ never found any tombs in the Valley of the Kings

Reading Skills | **Chronological Order**

✓ **Check-Up** Fill in the blanks according to the article.

1 The Egyptians started burying _____ in the Valley of the Kings in the 16th century B.C.
2 Howard Carter found the tomb of King _____ in 1922.
3 The most famous King Tut exhibition was in _____.

• **Exercise 6** •

Washington Crosses the Delaware

🎧 01-07

The American Revolution began badly in 1775. The first months were very hard. At first, many colonists wanted to give up on the war. During the winter of 1776, General George Washington had an idea. He wanted to win a great battle. He believed it would encourage the Americans.

It was Christmas night on December 25, 1776. Washington led 2,400 men across the Delaware River. He wanted to attack 1,500 German troops. They were fighting for the British. The Americans quietly sailed across the river. The Germans did not see them. The battle began. It ended quickly. After one and a half hours, the Germans surrendered. This victory made the Americans keep fighting. And they won the war in 1781.

battle n a fight
encourage v to give someone courage
surrender v to give up; to quit

Q1 According to paragraph 1, what is true of the American Revolution?
- Ⓐ Most Americans did not want to fight it.
- Ⓑ George Washington started it.
- Ⓒ It started badly for the Americans.
- Ⓓ There were just a few great battles.

Q2 According to paragraph 1, Washington fought the Germans because
- Ⓐ he wanted to encourage the Americans to continue fighting
- Ⓑ he thought he could completely surprise the Germans
- Ⓒ he had to sail across the Delaware River to attack them
- Ⓓ he wanted to win the American Revolution very quickly

Reading Skills | **Chronological Order**

✓ **Check-Up** Fill in the blanks according to the article.

1 The American Revolution began in _____. 2 George Washington led his men across the Delaware River on _____, _____. 3 The Americans won the war against the British in _____.

Exercise 7

Athenian Democracy

🎧 01-08

In the ancient world, most places had kings. The kings ruled the land. But one place was different. Athens was a city-state in Greece. The people there lived under a democracy. But in Athenian democracy, only adult male citizens could vote. So it was not a true democracy. Still, it was better than other places. Many people created Athens' democracy. The Athenian men all helped decide the actions Athens took.

First, Solon helped develop democracy around 594 B.C. He was the first to make changes. But there were many other great leaders. Cleisthenes expanded democracy in 508 B.C. Pericles was the greatest Athenian of all. He led Athens from around 461 to 429 B.C. Sadly, Athens did not stay a democracy. In 322 B.C., the Macedonians ended democracy there.

ancient adj very old
decide v to choose; to make a decision
expand v to make bigger; to make larger

Q1 According to paragraph 1, what is true of Athenian democracy?
- Ⓐ It was a real democracy.
- Ⓑ Its leader was always a king.
- Ⓒ Only some men could vote.
- Ⓓ The kings decided the government's actions.

Q2 In paragraph 2, the author's description of Solon mentions which of the following?
- Ⓐ The year he helped develop democracy
- Ⓑ His relationship with Cleisthenes
- Ⓒ The changes he made in Athens
- Ⓓ The years of his birth and death

Reading Skills | **Chronological Order**

✓ **Check-Up** Fill in the blanks according to the article.

1. _____ helped create democracy in 594 B.C.
2. Cleisthenes expanded democracy in _____.
3. _____ led Athens from around 461 to 429 B.C.
4. The _____ ended democracy in Athens in 322 B.C.

• Exercise 8 •

The Byzantine Empire

01-09

The Byzantine Empire was founded in the fourth century. Its capital was Constantinople. That is the city of Istanbul, Turkey, today. The empire was once very strong. It also controlled a great amount of land. It ruled much of Southeastern Europe and Turkey. It also ruled other parts of Europe, Africa, and the Middle East.

The empire lasted for more than 1,000 years. It had many great rulers. The first was Constantine the Great. Later, Justinian the Great was emperor. He ruled from 527 to 565. For a long time, the empire kept invaders out of Europe. But the Turks became very strong. After many years of war, they captured the capital. So the empire ended. This happened in 1453.

found v to start; to establish
capital n the city in a country where the main government is

Q1 In paragraph 1, the author's description of the Byzantine Empire mentions which of the following?
- Ⓐ How long it lasted
- Ⓑ Who founded it
- Ⓒ Where it was located
- Ⓓ What language it used

Q2 According to paragraph 2, why did the Byzantine Empire end?
- Ⓐ Justinian the Great lost a war.
- Ⓑ It was defeated by the Turks.
- Ⓒ Its government had bad rulers.
- Ⓓ Constantine the Great conquered it.

Reading Skills Chronological Order

Check-Up Insert a number from 1 to 4 in the correct order according to the article.

_____ Justinian the Great was the Byzantine emperor.
_____ The Turks captured Constantinople.
_____ Constantine the Great ruled the Byzantine Empire.
_____ There was a long period of war.

Grammar Point

Nouns

1 **Common nouns** are the names of any people, places, things, and ideas. **Proper nouns** are the names of people, places, and things. They always begin with capital letters.

Common Nouns
- He took the **bus** to **school**.
- The **dog** is eating a **bone**.
- They are going to the **park**.

Proper Nouns
- **Allen** is speaking with **John**.
- I live in the **United States**.
- Do you live in **Paris** or **Berlin**?

○ Read the following. The words in **bold** are proper nouns, and the ones in *italics* are common nouns.

> Hello, **Jennifer**.
> I am having a great *time* at the *beach* here in **Florida**. My *family* and I went to **Disneyworld** yesterday, and we rode on the *roller coasters*. We are going to **Miami** tomorrow. I hope that you are also enjoying your *vacation*. I can't wait to see you and **Sally**.
> **Lisa**

2 **Countable nouns** are things, people, and animals that we can count. They have plural forms. **Uncountable nouns** are things we cannot count, such as water, milk, and sugar. They do not have plural forms and do not use *a* or *an*.

Countable Nouns
- The **monkey** has ten **bananas**.
- I have two **tests** next week.

Uncountable Nouns
- Put some **milk** in my **coffee**.
- The **rain** is falling very hard.

○ Read the following. The words in **bold** are countable nouns, and the ones in *italics* are uncountable nouns.

> *John* went to the **zoo** yesterday. First, he saw some **monkeys**. They were eating lots of **bananas**. Then, he saw the **zebras**. They were just eating some *grass*. The **lions** and the **tigers** were all busy eating some *meat*. All the **animals** were eating, so *John* got hungry, too. He visited the **restaurant**. He got some *milk* and **cookies**. After he ate, he went downtown and met his **friends**.

Grammar Check-Up

A Circle the proper nouns and underline the common nouns.

building	river	archaeologist	Egypt	Solon
democracy	general	America	Civil War	tomb
Athens	capital	people	mountain	Chinese

B Complete the story with the best words in the box.

space   rockets   Soviet Union   moon   Apollo

In the 1960s, the United States and the _____ were trying to put a man on the moon. They sent _____ into outer _____. In July 1969, the United States launched _____ 11. On July 20, Neil Armstrong became the first man to walk on the _____ .

C Check the correct sentences.

1 ☐ Put some sugars in the iced tea.
2 ☐ I have ten fingers and ten toes.
3 ☐ There are too many car on the road.
4 ☐ He is putting on his shoes now.
5 ☐ The air in the city is very dirty.
6 ☐ We saw some deers in the forest.

D Circle the correct words.

1 Jason caught some (fish / fishes) at the lake.
2 May I borrow (pencil / a pencil) from you?
3 She loves to play in the (snow / snows).
4 Mark drank two bottles of (soda / sodas) at lunch.
5 His father sells (automobile / automobiles).

Vocabulary Review

A Circle the words that best complete the sentences.

1 Mount Everest is the (foreign / **highest**) mountain in the world.
2 (**Archaeologists** / Leaders) are people who study ancient cultures.
3 The (**pharaohs** / citizens) used to rule Egypt.
4 All the people can (expand / **vote**) in a democracy.
5 The men (**sailed** / climbed) across the river in a boat.

B Choose the best words to complete the sentences.

1 The country was _____ hundreds of years ago.
   Ⓐ decided
   Ⓑ changed
   Ⓒ founded
   Ⓓ kept

2 Since they lost the battle, the soldiers _____ to the enemy.
   Ⓐ surrendered
   Ⓑ invaded
   Ⓒ attacked
   Ⓓ protected

3 She liked to sit in the chair because it was _____.
   Ⓐ royal
   Ⓑ famous
   Ⓒ ancient
   Ⓓ comfortable

4 The _____ left their country and went to live in another one.
   Ⓐ voters
   Ⓑ treasures
   Ⓒ colonists
   Ⓓ archaeologists

5 The king _____ over the land for a period of many years.
   Ⓐ expanded
   Ⓑ ruled
   Ⓒ voted
   Ⓓ practiced

C Choose the words with the closest meanings to the highlighted words.

1. The people buried their leaders in tombs.
   - Ⓐ valleys
   - Ⓑ graves
   - Ⓒ countries
   - Ⓓ treasures

2. The general and his army defeated the enemy troops.
   - Ⓐ won against
   - Ⓑ fought
   - Ⓒ battled
   - Ⓓ assassinated

3. The contest began right at three o'clock.
   - Ⓐ expanded
   - Ⓑ invaded
   - Ⓒ commenced
   - Ⓓ explored

4. The historians were studying ancient cultures.
   - Ⓐ old
   - Ⓑ unique
   - Ⓒ different
   - Ⓓ foreign

5. The mountains in that country are very high.
   - Ⓐ valleys
   - Ⓑ rivers
   - Ⓒ walls
   - Ⓓ peaks

D Complete the sentences by filling in the blanks with the best words from the list. Change the forms of the words if necessary. Use each word only once.

> battle   robber   slave   expand   invaders

1. The _____ were trying to steal all the money from him.
2. There are no plans to _____ the local airport.
3. The _____ took over the city in just a few days.
4. The two armies fought a(n) _____ for several hours yesterday.
5. The _____ managed to escape and became a free person.

Chapter ❶   27

Practice Test

George Washington

George Washington was one of the greatest Americans in the country's history. During his lifetime, he did many things. He was a successful farmer. He was a statesman. He led the American army to victory in the Revolutionary War against Great Britain. He was also the first president of the United States.

As president, Washington helped set many examples for the later leaders of the country. These precedents were very important. So other men often followed Washington's examples.

Many early Americans despised kings. They were afraid the U.S. might become a monarchy as well. Many Americans wanted Washington to become king though. He, however, refused to be a king. Instead, he only served two terms as president. Then, he retired. For almost 150 years, all other presidents followed his example. They served only either one or two terms. The only man to serve more than two terms was Franklin D. Roosevelt. He was president from 1932 to 1945.

Washington also warned the country to be careful about getting involved in foreign affairs. The country has fought in many wars. But many Americans are isolationists. They do not really care about foreign events. Several presidents followed Washington's example as well. In this way, Washington was one of the most influential of all American presidents.

precedent n an example; a pattern
monarchy n a kingdom; a land with a king as its ruler

1. According to paragraph 1, which of the following is NOT true of George Washington?

    Ⓐ He was once a farmer.
    Ⓑ He served in the military.
    Ⓒ He was the leader of Great Britain.
    Ⓓ He was a great American.

2. Which of the following can be inferred from paragraph 2 about George Washington?

    Ⓐ He was the best president of the country.
    Ⓑ People usually ignored his precedents.
    Ⓒ He taught many later leaders of the country.
    Ⓓ People did not always follow his examples.

3. According to paragraph 3, many Americans thought

    Ⓐ Franklin Roosevelt was a good president
    Ⓑ Washington should become a king
    Ⓒ presidents should only serve two terms
    Ⓓ all presidents should follow Washington's examples

4. Which of the sentences below best expresses the essential information in the highlighted sentence in the passage? *Incorrect* answer choices change the meaning in important ways or leave out essential information.

    Ⓐ Washington thought the people should get involved with other countries.
    Ⓑ Washington believed foreign affairs were not very important.
    Ⓒ Washington warned people to get involved with only a few foreign countries.
    Ⓓ Washington wanted America to be cautious in issues with other countries.

5. The word "influential" in the passage is closest in meaning to

    Ⓐ important
    Ⓑ interesting
    Ⓒ creative
    Ⓓ unique

6 *Directions:* An introductory sentence for a brief summary of the passage is provided below. Complete the summary by selecting the THREE answer choices that express the most important ideas in the passage. Some answer choices do not belong in the summary because they express ideas that are not presented in the passage or are minor ideas in the passage. *This question is worth 2 points.*

George Washington was one of the most important people in the history of the United States.

-
-
-

Answer Choices

1. No one served more than two terms as president for 150 years.
2. Washington set many examples for future leaders.
3. Many people wanted Washington to become king.
4. Washington had a farm in the state of Virginia.
5. Washington helped defeat Great Britain in war.
6. Washington influenced many people in the country.

CHAPTER

02

Geography
(Comparison and Contrast)

① Great Rivers
② Australia and Greenland
③ Streams and Creeks
④ Canyons
⑤ The Earth's Poles
⑥ Deserts
⑦ Mountain Ranges
⑧ Korea and Japan

CHAPTER 2 **Geography** (Comparison and Contrast)

Understanding TOEFL Question Types & Reading Skills

1 Question Types — Negative Factual Questions

Negative Factual questions ask you to confirm correct information in the passage and then to find the information that is NOT true. One of the answer choices will have incorrect information. This is the correct answer. Pay attention to the facts in the passage. Make sure you can find the answer choice that is incorrect.

- **Example Negative Factual Questions**
  - According to the passage, which of the following is NOT true of X?
  - The author's description of X mentions all of the following EXCEPT:
  - In paragraph 2, all of the following questions are answered EXCEPT:

- **Useful Tips for Your Success**

Pay attention to	→	the facts in the entire passage.
	→	answer choices with information not in the passage.
Don't	→	choose an answer choice with information not from the passage.
	→	choose any answers mentioned in the passage.

Sample Question

Valleys

Valleys are lowlands. There are glacial and river valleys. Glacial valleys form from slow-moving ice. But river valleys form from moving water. River valleys form faster than glacial valleys. The bottoms of glacial valleys are wide. But those of river valleys are narrow.

02-01

glacial adj related to glaciers
form v to create; to come into being

Q According to the passage, which of the following is NOT true of valleys?
- Ⓐ Some valleys form quickly.
- Ⓑ Ice can form some valleys.
- Ⓒ There are two types of valleys.
- Ⓓ Glacial valleys are narrow.

2 Reading Skills — Comparison and Contrast

Comparing two or more things shows their similarities. Contrasting two or more things shows their differences. By using comparison and contrast, writers can show relationships between two or more things. Writers often use words like *more*, *less*, *as ... as*, and *the same as* to make comparisons and contrasts.

Check-Up

▶ Which comparison between glacial valleys and river valleys is accurate?
- Ⓐ Glacial valleys form faster than river valleys.
- Ⓑ Glacial valleys form the same way as river valleys.
- Ⓒ River valleys form quicker than glacial valleys.
- Ⓓ The bottoms of river valleys are wider than the bottoms of glacial valleys.

• **Exercise 1** •

Great Rivers

The Nile and Amazon are two of the world's great rivers. They are the largest in the world. But the Nile is longer than the Amazon. It is in Africa. The Amazon is in South America. Both rivers begin high in the mountains. The Nile flows south to north through a desert. However, the Amazon flows west to east through a rainforest.

great adj huge; large
rainforest n a tropical forest

Q The author's description of the Amazon River mentions all of the following EXCEPT:

Ⓐ the type of desert it flows through
Ⓑ the continent it is located in
Ⓒ the place where it begins
Ⓓ the direction that it flows

Reading Skills **Comparison and Contrast**

Check-Up For the sentences, write "D" for difference or "S" for similarity in the blanks.

1 _____ The Nile and the Amazon are two very large rivers.
2 _____ The Nile is in Africa, but the Amazon is in South America.
3 _____ The Amazon flows west to east, but the Nile flows south to north.
4 _____ Both the Nile and the Amazon begin in the mountains.

• **Exercise 2** •

Australia and Greenland

02-03

Australia and Greenland are two large landmasses. Some people believe Australia is the Earth's largest island. But they are incorrect. It is not an island. It is a continent. That means Greenland is the largest island in the world. Many people live in Australia. But few people reside in Greenland. Greenland's weather is usually cold. But Australia's is much warmer.

landmass n a large area of land
reside v to live

Q According to the passage, which of the following is NOT true of Australia?

Ⓐ It has many people.
Ⓑ It is a continent.
Ⓒ It is smaller than Greenland.
Ⓓ It is much warmer than Greenland.

Reading Skills | **Comparison and Contrast**

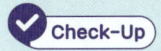 Which comparison between Australia and Greenland is accurate?

Ⓐ Greenland has more people than Australia.
Ⓑ Australia is as large as Greenland.
Ⓒ Greenland is a larger island than Australia.
Ⓓ Australia's weather is warmer than Greenland's weather.

• **Exercise 3** •

Streams and Creeks

 02-04

    Both streams and creeks are bodies of water. People often believe they are the same. But they are actually different. Streams are longer than creeks. Streams also have more water than creeks. Sometimes creeks have no water. But streams always have flowing water. Finally, you can operate a boat on a stream. But you cannot use a boat on a creek.

flow v to move; to run
operate v to use and control

Q In the passage, all of the following questions are answered EXCEPT:

   Ⓐ How deep are creeks?
   Ⓑ Which is the longer body of water?
   Ⓒ What can you operate on a stream?
   Ⓓ Which body of water sometimes has no water?

Reading Skills **Comparison and Contrast**

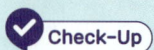 **Check-Up** For the sentences, write "D" for difference or "S" for similarity in the blanks.

  1 _____ Streams always have flowing water, but creeks do not.
  2 _____ Streams and creeks both have water in them.
  3 _____ Creeks are shorter than streams.
  4 _____ People can operate boats on streams, but they cannot do that on creeks.

• **Exercise 4** •

Canyons

    A canyon is a narrow, deep valley. It is formed by a river. Over a long period of time, the flowing water erodes the land. This creates the canyon. Most canyons have very steep sides. Some, like the Grand Canyon, can be thousands of feet deep. Not all canyons are on land. Some are underwater. These are also formed by water erosion.

valley [n] the area between two or more mountains
steep [adj] being almost vertical

Q According to the passage, which of the following is NOT true of canyons?
   Ⓐ Rivers create them.
   Ⓑ They form very quickly.
   Ⓒ They can be under the water.
   Ⓓ They are narrow and deep.

Reading Skills   **Comparison and Contrast**

✓ Check-Up   Which comparison between canyons on land and canyons underwater is accurate?

   Ⓐ Both of them can be very wide.
   Ⓑ Both of them were formed by erosion.
   Ⓒ Canyons on land are deeper than underwater canyons.
   Ⓓ Underwater canyons form faster than canyons on land.

• **Exercise 5** •

The Earth's Poles

02-06

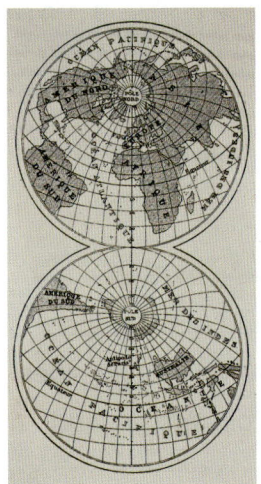

The North and South poles are at opposite ends of the Earth. Both places are extremely isolated and cold. But the South Pole can get colder than the North Pole. The North Pole is the northernmost place on the Earth. Its location is the Arctic. Meanwhile, the South Pole is the southernmost point on the Earth. Its location is the Antarctic.

The North Pole is actually in the middle of the Arctic Ocean. But the South Pole is on land. Both poles have great amounts of ice. But the ice at the South Pole is thicker than the ice at the North Pole.

For a long time, people dreamed of reaching both poles. An expedition eventually reached the North Pole before the South Pole.

opposite adj different; opposed
isolated adj separate; cut off
eventually adv finally; ultimately

Q1 In paragraph 1, all of the following questions are answered EXCEPT:
Ⓐ Where is the South Pole located?
Ⓑ Which pole has colder weather?
Ⓒ What is the weather like at the North Pole?
Ⓓ How many people have visited the North Pole?

Q2 According to the passage, which of the following is NOT true of the North Pole?
Ⓐ It is opposite the South Pole.
Ⓑ It is not as cold as the South Pole.
Ⓒ Its location is the Antarctic.
Ⓓ It is in the middle of an ocean.

Reading Skills **Comparison and Contrast**

 **For the sentences, write "D" for difference or "S" for similarity in the blanks.**

1 _____ The South Pole has thicker ice than the North Pole.
2 _____ The South Pole is on land, but the North Pole is on the water.
3 _____ The North and South poles are both very cold.
4 _____ Expeditions have reached both the North Pole and the South Pole.

• **Exercise 6** •

Deserts

Some people suppose that all deserts are hot. However, this is not accurate. The planet also has some cold deserts. The Sahara Desert in Africa is an example of a hot desert. Antarctica is the largest cold desert in the world. Actually, Antarctica is bigger than the Sahara. In fact, it is a gigantic continent.

The Sahara is just one part of a continent. It contains a lot of sand and is windy. But the cold deserts of Antarctica have lots of snow and ice. The Sahara is the hottest area on the Earth. Antarctica is the coldest region in the world. Finally, Antarctica does not have any bodies of water. But the Sahara does. These bodies of water are oases.

planet n a world; a globe
gigantic adj extremely large; huge
oasis n a place in the desert with water; a sanctuary; a safe place

Q1 The author's description of the Sahara Desert mentions all of the following EXCEPT:

Ⓐ its size in comparison with Antarctica
Ⓑ how hot the temperature gets there
Ⓒ what the bodies of water in it are called
Ⓓ where it is located

Q2 According to the passage, which of the following is NOT true of Antarctica?

Ⓐ It is a large continent.
Ⓑ It is an example of a cold desert.
Ⓒ It is not the coldest place on the Earth.
Ⓓ It has no bodies of water.

Reading Skills | Comparison and Contrast

Check-Up Which comparison between the Sahara Desert and Antarctica is accurate?

Ⓐ The Sahara Desert is larger than Antarctica.
Ⓑ Antarctica has more bodies of water than the Sahara Desert.
Ⓒ The Sahara Desert is colder than Antarctica.
Ⓓ The Sahara Desert has more sand than Antarctica.

• **Exercise 7** •

Mountain Ranges

Two well-known mountain ranges are the Himalayas and the Appalachians. Interestingly, they are very dissimilar from each other.

The Himalayas are mainly in Nepal in Asia. But they are also in other countries such as China and India. They have some of the highest peaks in the world. They formed about seventy million years ago. And they are still growing.

The Appalachians are in the United States. They are not as high or as dangerous as the Himalayas. In fact, their peaks are fairly low. So climbing them is easy. This is very different from the Himalayas. The Appalachians formed nearly 300 million years ago. So they are much older than the Himalayas. They ceased growing a long time ago.

dissimilar adj different; unlike
mainly adv primarily; mostly
cease v to stop; to quit

Q1 In paragraph 2, all of the following questions are answered EXCEPT:
Ⓐ How long ago did the Himalayas form?
Ⓑ Which countries are the Himalayas found in?
Ⓒ What continent are the Himalayas located in?
Ⓓ When did the Himalayas stop growing?

Q2 According to paragraph 3, which of the following is NOT true of the Appalachians?
Ⓐ They are older than the Himalayas.
Ⓑ They are not as high as the Himalayas.
Ⓒ They are not very easy to climb.
Ⓓ They are in the United States.

Reading Skills **Comparison and Contrast**

Check-Up For the sentences, write "D" for difference or "S" for similarity in the blanks.

1 _____ The Himalayas and the Appalachians are both mountain ranges.
2 _____ The Himalayas are growing, but the Appalachians are not.
3 _____ The Appalachians and the Himalayas both formed many millions of years ago.
4 _____ The Himalayas are very high, but the Appalachians are not.

• **Exercise 8** •

Korea and Japan

Korea and Japan are both countries in Northeast Asia. But they have some differences. For example, Korea is a peninsula. So water surrounds it on three sides. But Japan is an island nation. It has four main islands. There are many smaller ones, too. Korea also has many islands.

At first glance, the countries seem to be very different. But they are actually similar to each other. They both have comparable climates. So they often get the same kinds of weather. Both of them get typhoons at the end of summer. The typhoons are usually stronger in Japan though. Both of them have extensive mountain ranges. But Japan has the highest mountain. It is Mount Fuji. Therefore, in several ways, they are quite similar.

peninsula n a body of land with water on three sides   **comparable** adj similar; equal
nation n a country; a state

Q1 The author's description of Korea mentions all of the following EXCEPT:
 Ⓐ where it can be found
 Ⓑ what kind of landform it is on
 Ⓒ how close it is to Japan
 Ⓓ how many of its sides water is on

Q2 According to the passage, which of the following is NOT true of Japan?
 Ⓐ Mount Fuji is in Japan.
 Ⓑ It has different weather from Korea.
 Ⓒ It often gets strong typhoons.
 Ⓓ It has many small islands.

Reading Skills   Comparison and Contrast

Check-Up Which comparison between Korea and Japan is accurate?

 Ⓐ Both Japan and Korea are island nations.
 Ⓑ Japan has a higher mountain than Korea.
 Ⓒ Korea has stronger typhoons than Japan.
 Ⓓ Both Japan and Korea have very high mountains.

Grammar Point — Adjectives

		Be Verb + Adjective + Preposition
Prepositions	Adjectives	Prepositional Phrases
at	good bad surprised excellent mad	• Eric is good at geography. • David is bad at math. • The teacher was surprised at her class. • Mr. Jenkins is excellent at foreign languages. • I am so mad at you right now.
about	anxious worried concerned happy annoyed	• Jerry is anxious about his grade on the test. • Craig is worried about his mother. • She is concerned about the price of that computer. • I am happy about your decision. • Larry was annoyed about losing the game.
of	afraid plenty short free sure	• Mary is afraid of ghosts. • There is plenty of pizza for everyone. • He is short of money. • The students are free of stress during vacation. • Kay is sure of her decision.
from	different	• This is very different from the Himalayas.
on	intent keen dependent based	• He is intent on finding his wallet. • They are keen on sports day. • Thomas is dependent on his mom. • That book is based on a true story.
to	similar equal addicted liable opposite	• People often believe they are similar to each other. • His height is equal to hers. • Pamela is addicted to chocolate • He is liable to leave the office early. • The result was opposite to our hopes.
with	pleased satisfied familiar obsessed busy	• Cynthia's dad was pleased with her test score. • Are you satisfied with the result? • Mark is familiar with that book. • He is obsessed with traveling abroad. • They are always busy with work.
for	known famous	• She is known for her generosity. • Italy is famous for its food.

Grammar Check-Up

A Circle the phrases that best complete the sentences.

1 My father was not (pleased with / obsessed with) my math grade.
2 Everyone was (surprised at / addicted to) Paul's ability to play basketball.
3 Scott is (busy with / afraid of) snakes, spiders, and fire.
4 Minho's answer is (different from / famous for) Eunjoo's answer.
5 Are you (plenty of / concerned about) tomorrow's final exam?

B Circle the parts of the sentences that are grammatically incorrect.

1 John was intent with getting to the party early.
　　　ⓐ　　ⓑ　　ⓒ　　ⓓ
2 Mountains and hills are very similar on each other.
　　　　　　　ⓐ　　　ⓑ　　ⓒ　　ⓓ
3 Do you remember what this city is know for?
　　　　　ⓐ　　　　ⓑ　　　　　　ⓒ　　ⓓ
4 All of the students are worried with their presentation tomorrow.
　ⓐ　　　　ⓑ　　　　ⓒ　　　ⓓ
5 They were obsessed to finding their way to the North Pole.
　　　　　　　ⓐ　　　ⓑ　　ⓒ　　ⓓ

C Choose the sentences that are NOT grammatically correct.

1 ⓐ That blockbuster movie is based on a book.
　ⓑ My brother is addicted to chocolate.
　ⓒ Joanie's teacher is very mad for her right now.
　ⓓ He is happy about his upcoming trip.

2 ⓐ Your ability is equal with his.
　ⓑ I am not familiar with this computer game.
　ⓒ You should not be surprised at my reaction.
　ⓓ I sat opposite to him during the meal.

3 ⓐ We were all annoyed about Allen's actions.
　ⓑ Taylor is not too keen on Physics.
　ⓒ I am not sure of my plans for this weekend.
　ⓓ I am a little short on time these days.

Vocabulary Review

A Circle the words that best complete the sentences.

1. Greg did not give an (accurate / opposite) answer to the test question.
2. The Amazon River is (longer / higher) than the Mississippi River.
3. The (climate / typhoon) in that country is fairly nice.
4. Antarctica has the largest (rainforest / desert) in the world.
5. There are only seven (islands / continents) on the Earth.

B Choose the best words to complete the sentences.

1. The Grand Canyon is extremely _____ at the top.
   - A well-known
   - B accurate
   - C wide
   - D thick

2. Korea and Florida are both _____ because they have water on three sides.
   - A islands
   - B peninsulas
   - C continents
   - D rainforests

3. Peter spoke _____ to his friends and not to any other people.
   - A actually
   - B extremely
   - C almost
   - D mainly

4. Water can _____ land and wash it away.
   - A erode
   - B avoid
   - C dry
   - D save

5. This hill is too _____ for people to climb.
   - A deep
   - B steep
   - C light
   - D strong

C Choose the words with the closest meanings to the highlighted words.

1. The factory has ceased making bicycles.
   - A had
   - B reached
   - C begun
   - D stopped

2. There are many lowlands in some parts of the United States.
   - A rivers
   - B valleys
   - C islands
   - D peninsulas

3. The doctor supposed that Mitch had the flu.
   - A believed
   - B dreamed
   - C operated
   - D flowed

4. Mr. Lee resides in an apartment in the suburbs.
   - A forms
   - B has
   - C contains
   - D lives

5. Greenland is a great island in the Atlantic Ocean.
   - A gigantic
   - B warm
   - C cold
   - D bigger

D Complete the sentences by filling in the blanks with the best words from the list. Change the forms of the words if necessary. Use each word only once.

| surround | landmass | narrow | stream | incorrect |

1. Water _____ an island on all of its sides.
2. The entrance to the valley is very _____ but then becomes wide later.
3. The student's answer on the test was _____.
4. The fishermen were on the _____ trying to catch some fish.
5. The largest _____ on the Earth is Asia.

Practice Test

Tundra

Tundra is a type of biome only found in areas that get extremely cold weather. It has two primary characteristics. The first is that the region must have frozen ground. The second is that there are no tall trees in it.

Much of the Earth's surface—around twenty percent—is tundra. Tundra can be flat land, yet it can also have mountains and hills. Many parts of Russia, Canada, Greenland, Northern Europe, and Alaska are considered tundra. The land in those places is called Arctic tundra. **1** It has cold weather all year long. **2** As a result, the ground just beneath the topsoil is permanently frozen. **3** This is known as permafrost. **4** In some places, the permafrost can be more than 450 meters deep.

Because the subsoil is frozen, trees cannot live in tundra. Their roots are unable to grow deep underground. The majority of plants in tundra are mosses and shrubs. Wildflowers also grow in some places. These plants all grow low to the ground. And their roots do not need to be too deep in the soil.

topsoil n the fertile upper part of the soil
root n the part of a plant that grows down into the soil

1   The word "primary" in the passage is closest in meaning to

    Ⓐ clear
    Ⓑ interesting
    Ⓒ known
    Ⓓ main

2   In paragraph 2, the author implies that tundra

    Ⓐ is a common biome on the Earth
    Ⓑ has no animals living in it
    Ⓒ is usually hilly or mountainous
    Ⓓ gets warm temperatures in summer

3   According to paragraph 2, which of the following is true of tundra?

    Ⓐ The topsoil in it is usually frozen.
    Ⓑ Almost all of Greenland is tundra.
    Ⓒ People are unable to live in it.
    Ⓓ It can have very deep permafrost.

4   In paragraph 3, the author uses "mosses and shrubs" as examples of

    Ⓐ the only types of plants in tundra
    Ⓑ plants that cannot grow in tundra
    Ⓒ common plants in tundra
    Ⓓ plants with deep roots

5   Look at the four squares [■] that indicate where the following sentence could be added to the passage.

    Alpine tundra is another type and is found in mountainous areas.

    Where would the sentence best fit?
    Click on a square [■] to add the sentence to the passage.

6 *Directions:* An introductory sentence for a brief summary of the passage is provided below. Complete the summary by selecting the THREE answer choices that express the most important ideas in the passage. Some answer choices do not belong in the summary because they express ideas that are not presented in the passage or are minor ideas in the passage. *This question is worth 2 points.*

Tundra is a unique type of biome on the Earth.

-
-
-

Answer Choices

1. The weather in tundra is very cold all year long.
2. Tundra is more common than any other biome on the Earth.
3. Only low-growing plants are found in tundra.
4. Some tundra has lots of mountains in it.
5. Some of the ground in tundra is frozen all year long.
6. Tundra can be found in many places in Antarctica.

CHAPTER 03

Technology
(Cause and Effect)

1. The Internet
2. Flying Cars
3. The Telegraph
4. The Concorde
5. The Industrial Revolution
6. Satellites
7. Gutenberg and the Printing Press
8. Thomas Edison

CHAPTER 3 Technology (Cause and Effect)

Understanding TOEFL Question Types & Reading Skills

1 Question Types — Inference Questions

Inference questions ask about arguments or ideas that the passage does not mention. The author implies these things but does not actually include them in the passage. Pay attention to the causes or effects of different arguments or ideas. Think about why something happened or why something will happen in the future.

- **Example Inference Questions**
    - Which of the following can be inferred about X?
    - The author of the passage implies that X ~
    - Which of the following can be inferred from paragraph 1 about X?

- **Useful Tips for Your Success**
    - Pay attention to → causes and effects.
        - → suggestions and results.
    - Don't → pick answers that contradict the main idea.
        - → choose answers just because they look right.

Sample Question

The Assembly Line

🎧 03-01

People used to manufacture products slowly. One person made all of a product's parts. But Henry Ford had an idea. He used the assembly line. Workers specialized in one part of manufacturing. So making different products became much faster.

manufacture v to make; to create
specialize v to focus on doing just one thing

Q The author of the passage implies that Henry Ford
- Ⓐ made his own products
- Ⓑ produced high-quality goods
- Ⓒ started the mass-production of items
- Ⓓ was a manufacturing specialist

2 Reading Skills — Cause and Effect

The cause is the reason something happened. The effect is the result of that action. By using cause and effect, writers can show how one action caused another. Writers often use words and phrases like *so*, *because*, *therefore*, *due to*, and *thanks to* to connect a cause and its effect.

Check-Up

▶ For the pair of sentences below, mark "C" for cause and "E" for effect.

_____ Making different products became much faster.

_____ Workers specialized in one part of manufacturing.

• **Exercise 1** •

The Internet

🎧 03-02

The Internet was one of the most crucial creations in the last over sixty years. The United States armed forces began making it by themselves in the 1960s. They were worried about nuclear war. So they wanted a secure method to contact people. Other groups have made many improvements to the Internet. Due to those advances, millions of people use the Internet every day.

crucial [adj] important; central
armed forces [n] the military

Q   Which of the following can be inferred about the United States armed forces?
Ⓐ They started a nuclear war in the 1960s.
Ⓑ They have made many changes to the Internet.
Ⓒ They invented the Internet to protect people.
Ⓓ They were not the only ones to work on the Internet.

Reading Skills   **Cause and Effect**

✓ **Check-Up** For each pair of sentences below, mark "C" for cause and "E" for effect.

1   _____ The armed forces were worried about nuclear war.
    _____ So the military wanted a secure method to contact people.
2   _____ Therefore millions of people use the Internet every day.
    _____ There have been many improvements to the Internet.

• Exercise 2 •

Flying Cars

🎧 03-03

People are always thinking about the future. They want to improve upon various inventions. So, today, many inventors are working on flying cars. Actually, there are already some flying cars. But they are too expensive now. They also use too much fuel. But someday they will be common. Therefore, many people will own them.

improve v to make better; to raise
actually adv really; in fact

Q Which of the following can be inferred from the passage about flying cars?

Ⓐ They are somewhat cheap now.
Ⓑ Only a few people own them.
Ⓒ Everyone wants to have one.
Ⓓ No one has invented them yet.

Reading Skills Cause and Effect

 **For each pair of sentences below, mark "C" for cause and "E" for effect.**

1 _____ So, today, many inventors are working on flying cars.
  _____ Inventors want to improve upon various inventions.

2 _____ Someday flying cars will be common.
  _____ Therefore, many people will own them.

• **Exercise 3** •

The Telegraph

03-04

In the mid-1800s, Samuel Morse invented the telegraph. It used electricity. It could send messages over wires. This changed how people communicated very much. Before, people sent letters. Those took a long time to be delivered. But telegraph messages were received fast. So people could talk instantly. The telegraph became very popular. People could even send messages across the ocean. This helped bring people closer together.

wire n a thin piece of metal that carries electricity
instantly adv at once; immediately

Q The author of the passage implies that the telegraph
- Ⓐ cost a lot of money to use
- Ⓑ was faster than sending a letter
- Ⓒ could work without a wire
- Ⓓ was easy to invent

Reading Skills Cause and Effect

 **Check-Up** For each pair of sentences below, mark "C" for cause and "E" for effect.

1 _____ So people could talk instantly.
   _____ Telegraph messages were received fast.
2 _____ People could even send messages across the ocean.
   _____ This helped bring people closer together.

• **Exercise 4** •

The Concorde

After the Wright brothers flew their first airplane, people began establishing airlines. Flying was much faster than driving or taking the train. Sailing across the Atlantic Ocean was especially slow. So companies from England and France developed the Concorde. The Concorde flew faster than the speed of sound. Therefore, people could cross the Atlantic from America to England in three hours instead of six.

establish v to create; to found
airline n a company that flies airplanes for people

Q Which of the following can be inferred about airplanes?

Ⓐ Most airplanes flew slower than the speed of sound.
Ⓑ The Wright brothers used them to create airlines.
Ⓒ They usually could not fly across the Atlantic Ocean.
Ⓓ The British and the French developed the first ones.

Reading Skills   Cause and Effect

Check-Up For each pair of sentences below, mark "C" for cause and "E" for effect.

1 _____ So companies from England and France developed the Concorde.
   _____ Sailing across the Atlantic Ocean was especially slow.

2 _____ The Concorde flew faster than the speed of sound.
   _____ Therefore, people could cross the Atlantic in three hours instead of six.

• **Exercise 5** •

The Industrial Revolution

For many centuries, men made few inventions. But in the eighteenth century, men suddenly began creating many new machines. People now call this era the Industrial Revolution. It began around the middle of the eighteenth century. And some people believe it is still going on.

There were many improvements in textiles. Richard Arkwright invented a new way to spin cotton. This was faster and more efficient than the old way. So this made clothes much cheaper. James Watt also invented the steam engine. Thanks to his creation, people could make better ships. People also designed trains to run on his engines. People also created better ways to make iron. This made iron stronger. So buildings were much higher in quality.

era n an important period in time **efficient** adj effective; capable
textile n fabric; cloth

Q1 In paragraph 1, the author implies that the Industrial Revolution
 Ⓐ was not very important
 Ⓑ only made iron better
 Ⓒ has not ended yet
 Ⓓ had few good inventions

Q2 Which of the following can be inferred from paragraph 2 about James Watt?
 Ⓐ He became a very rich man.
 Ⓑ He helped improve transportation.
 Ⓒ He owned a shipping company.
 Ⓓ He invented the first train.

Reading Skills | **Cause and Effect**

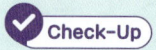 **Check-Up** Which sentence group below does NOT show cause and effect?

 Ⓐ James Watt also invented the steam engine. People could make better ships.
 Ⓑ People created better ways to make iron. This made iron stronger.
 Ⓒ This was faster and more efficient than the old way. This made clothes much cheaper.
 Ⓓ The Industrial Revolution began around the middle of the eighteenth century. And some people believe the Industrial Revolution is still going on.

• **Exercise 6** •

Satellites

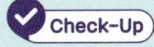 03-07

In 1957, the USSR (Union of Soviet Socialist Republics) launched *Sputnik*. This was the world's first satellite. It only stayed in orbit for a short time. Nevertheless, people realized that satellites could be very important. So now there are hundreds of satellites orbiting the Earth. Governments, militaries, and companies send satellites into space. They do this for themselves for many reasons.

Some satellites watch the weather. They can see much of the Earth. So they can predict the weather very well. They can also see many changes in weather patterns. Other satellites help with communications. They help with telephone calls and Internet connections. So people can contact one another cheaply and conveniently. And other satellites spy on countries. Militaries use these. So they can watch other countries' armies and navies.

orbit v to circle around a planet or star
predict v to guess; to make a guess about the future
conveniently adv easily; comfortably

Q1 According to paragraph 1, which of the following can be inferred about satellites?
- Ⓐ They always operate in space.
- Ⓑ They are expensive to build.
- Ⓒ They are not particularly useful.
- Ⓓ Only the USSR has launched them.

Q2 In paragraph 2, the author implies that Internet connections
- Ⓐ are common on spy satellites
- Ⓑ are always fairly expensive
- Ⓒ are helpful to communications
- Ⓓ can help predict the weather

Reading Skills **Cause and Effect**

Check-Up Which sentence group below does NOT show cause and effect?

- Ⓐ This was the world's first satellite. It only stayed in orbit for a short time.
- Ⓑ Satellites can see much of the Earth. They can predict the weather very well.
- Ⓒ People realized that satellites could be very important. Now there are hundreds of satellites orbiting the Earth.
- Ⓓ Satellites help with telephone calls and Internet connections. People can contact one another cheaply and conveniently.

• **Exercise 7** •

Gutenberg and the Printing Press

For most of history, few people could read. Books were extremely rare. They were incredibly expensive and also took many months or years to create. But one man made books available to everyone.

Johannes Gutenberg lived in Germany during the fifteenth century. He was a printer and goldsmith. He realized books were difficult to make. Thus he created movable type. This process enabled people to make books quickly. So books became cheaper.

Gutenberg's printing press spread throughout Europe. Soon, people were printing hundreds of books. More people could therefore buy these cheap books. People also learned to read. That improved knowledge in Europe. Thanks to the printing press, a rebirth of knowledge occurred throughout Europe. People called this period the Renaissance.

extremely adv very; tremendously
goldsmith n a person who makes things from gold
rebirth n renewal; a revival

Q1 Which of the following can be inferred from paragraph 1 about books?
- Ⓐ They were usually quite big.
- Ⓑ Very few people owned them.
- Ⓒ People wrote them very quickly.
- Ⓓ People often read them out loud.

Q2 In paragraphs 2 and 3, the author implies that Johannes Gutenberg
- Ⓐ became a rich man
- Ⓑ lived in many different places
- Ⓒ wrote the first cheap book
- Ⓓ helped start the Renaissance

Reading Skills | **Cause and Effect**

 Which sentence group below does NOT show cause and effect?

- Ⓐ Johannes Gutenberg lived in Germany during the fifteenth century. He was a printer and goldsmith.
- Ⓑ Soon, people were printing hundreds of books. More people could buy these cheap books.
- Ⓒ Gutenberg realized books were difficult to make. Thus he created movable type.
- Ⓓ People also learned to read. That improved knowledge in Europe.

• Exercise 8 •

Thomas Edison

One of history's greatest inventors was Thomas Edison. Strangely, at first, people thought he was stupid. He only went to school for three months. But Edison worked hard. Therefore, he accomplished many great things.

Edison held patents for more than 1,000 inventions. One of his first inventions was the phonograph. This machine amazed people. It could play back sounds and music.

However, Edison's most famous invention was the electric light bulb. He actually did not invent the first light bulb. He invented the first commercially usable light bulb. Thanks to the light bulb, people's lives changed. They stayed awake later. They could do more nighttime activities. They also did not have to depend upon gas or wood for light.

stupid adj not smart or intelligent; idiotic
patent n the legal right to an invention
depend upon phr to rely upon

Q1 According to the passage, which of the following can be inferred about Thomas Edison?
- Ⓐ He graduated from college.
- Ⓑ He was not intelligent.
- Ⓒ He learned things by himself.
- Ⓓ He wanted to become rich.

Q2 Which of the following can be inferred from paragraph 3 about the light bulb?
- Ⓐ It was not efficient at first.
- Ⓑ It made Edison very famous.
- Ⓒ It used gas to make light.
- Ⓓ It gave people new lifestyles.

Reading Skills Cause and Effect

 **Check-Up** Which sentence group below does NOT show cause and effect?

- Ⓐ Thanks to the light bulb, people's lives changed. They stayed awake later.
- Ⓑ They stayed awake later. They could do more nighttime activities.
- Ⓒ Edison held patents for more than 1,000 inventions. One of his first inventions was the phonograph.
- Ⓓ Edison worked hard. He accomplished many great things.

Grammar Point

Pronouns

Expressions with Pronouns

Expressions	Synonyms	Example Sentences
and all that	and so on	• There was plenty of ice cream, jellies, and all that. • I'm fed up with work, meetings, and all that.
that is to say	in other words	• That is to say, I'm not really sure. • That is to say, this is very confusing.
all the same	nevertheless	• All the same, I don't want to do it. • All the same, it will be very difficult.
same here	I agree / me, too	• A: I want to eat now. B: Same here. • A: I think we should stop working. B: Same here.
one after another	in a row	• He lined up the dominoes one after another. • She saw the cars go by one after another.
one after the other	consecutively	• Everyone came one after the other. • She drank three cups of water one after the other.
for oneself	without others' help	• She bought a car for herself. • John prepared dinner for himself.
of oneself	automatically	• The door opened of itself. • The boat sailed away of itself.
by oneself	alone	• I went to the party by myself. • Lisa often studies by herself.
in itself	by nature	• Its existence is a miracle in itself. • Your success is amazing in itself.
to oneself	exclusively	• Kevin was speaking to himself. • Why are you doing this to yourself?
come to oneself	to become conscious	• When he came to himself, he raised his head. • She came to herself and started acting normally.
beside oneself	angry	• She was beside herself with anger. • I was beside myself with anger.
between ourselves	confidentially	• Let's keep this news between ourselves. • They kept that secret between themselves.

Grammar Check-Up

A Complete the sentences by using the given words.

1 Can you give _____ (I) something to drink?
2 Jenny did the report all by _____ (she).
3 _____ (He) does not want to go to school today.
4 Is this mine or _____ (you)?
5 I talked to _____ (they) about our problems.

B Choose the correct words for each blank.

1 _____, I guess that we can do it.
   ⓐ By myself   ⓑ One after another   ⓒ Same here   ⓓ All the same

2 Sometimes I like to eat all _____.
   ⓐ of yourself   ⓑ by myself   ⓒ for myself   ⓓ in itself

3 We need to keep this secret _____.
   ⓐ all the same   ⓑ for ourselves   ⓒ between ourselves   ⓓ beside ourselves

4 The sheep all went into the barn _____.
   ⓐ that is to say   ⓑ one after the other   ⓒ beside themselves   ⓓ for themselves

5 You should not sing _____ all the time. It's annoying.
   ⓐ of yourself   ⓑ and all that   ⓒ beside yourself   ⓓ to yourself

C Read the following story and fill in the blanks with the pronouns in the box. Use each word only once.

> they   one after the other   all the same   them   it   my   beside themselves

I often meet _____ friends on the weekend. We usually go to the park and play some games. Last weekend, there were some other people in the park. _____ were playing soccer together. My friends wanted to play too, so we asked _____ to join their game. The other team agreed, so we all played together. My friend Steve scored three goals _____. _____ was really amazing. The other team was _____ with anger when they lost. _____, everyone had a great time. Maybe we will meet them again in the future and play another game together.

Vocabulary Review

A Circle the words that best complete the sentences.

1 The moon (makes / orbits) Earth every twenty-nine days.
2 The (connection / government) was bad, so John could not hear the caller very well.
3 The intelligent student had a lot of (knowledge / inventors).
4 The military sent some (phones / satellites) into outer space.
5 Thomas Edison made many important (inventions / processes) throughout his life.

B Choose the best words to complete the sentences.

1 Lisa could run _____ than everyone else in her class.
  A later
  B expensive
  C greatest
  D faster

2 The weatherman _____ it would rain on the weekend.
  A specialized
  B predicted
  C contacted
  D changed

3 The scientist made many _____ to the computer to make it better.
  A inventors
  B creations
  C improvements
  D presses

4 Nowadays, everyone has books, so they are very _____.
  A rare
  B expensive
  C common
  D better

5 Nobody _____ that the answer to the question was incorrect.
  A realized
  B made
  C improved
  D used

C Choose the words with the closest meanings to the highlighted words.

1 There were many various kinds of animals at the zoo.
   - Ⓐ different
   - Ⓑ stupid
   - Ⓒ crucial
   - Ⓓ secure

2 Harry tried very hard to improve his grade in the class.
   - Ⓐ raise
   - Ⓑ realize
   - Ⓒ establish
   - Ⓓ make

3 The company specialized in making textiles.
   - Ⓐ airplanes
   - Ⓑ trains
   - Ⓒ fabrics
   - Ⓓ inventions

4 The man was incredibly interested in learning about the subject.
   - Ⓐ easily
   - Ⓑ conveniently
   - Ⓒ finally
   - Ⓓ extremely

5 The company develops many new products every year.
   - Ⓐ prints
   - Ⓑ creates
   - Ⓒ works
   - Ⓓ contacts

D Complete the sentences by filling in the blanks with the best words from the list. Change the forms of the words if necessary. Use each word only once.

> enable   future   specialize   spin   launch

1 Your help _____ me to finish my work yesterday.
2 That engineer currently _____ in computers.
3 The space agency will _____ the rocket in about two hours.
4 The top is _____ around and around in circles.
5 No one knows what the _____ will be like.

Practice Test

The Benefits of the Space Program

Many people in the United States dislike the space program. They believe the government should spend more money for people on the Earth. They claim the space program has few benefits. However, they are quite wrong. The space program has actually helped people in many ways.

First, astronomers have learned many things about the moon, planets, solar system, and stars. So basic human knowledge has improved. Many satellites have also sent back information to the Earth about the planets and other galaxies. These are some benefits of the space program.

Second, it has even affected the lives of regular people. This is due to the technological advances scientists have made. First of all, satellites enable people to watch cable TV and to use their cellphones. Satellites can even help predict the weather. Scientists in the space program also first invented cordless technology. So nowadays, many different pieces of equipment do not use cords.

Furthermore, there have been medical advances. For example, many people have laser surgery. Scientists in the space program first developed this technology. Even body imaging like in CAT scans and MRIs comes from space advances.

Clearly, the space program has benefited many people. It has not just helped scientists and astronauts. Instead, it has helped regular individuals as well.

enable v to allow; to make possible
predict v to guess; to know in advance

1 According to paragraph 1, which of the following is true of the space program?

   (A) It costs too much money.
   (B) It has very few uses.
   (C) Everyone in the United States dislikes it.
   (D) It has benefited many people.

2 Which of the sentences below best expresses the essential information in the highlighted sentence in the passage? *Incorrect* answer choices change the meaning in important ways or leave out essential information.

   (A) Astronomers know everything about the moon, planets, solar system, and stars.
   (B) Experts are teaching people about some of the many different objects in outer space.
   (C) Astronomers have learned a lot about many of the different objects in outer space.
   (D) Scientists want to know more about the moon, planets, solar system, and stars.

3 Why does the author mention "cordless technology" in paragraph 3?

   (A) To claim that it is better than other technology
   (B) To provide a benefit of the space program
   (C) To compare it with cable TV and cellphones
   (D) To discuss a medical use of space technology

4 In paragraph 4, the author implies that lasers

   (A) are the most effective in outer space
   (B) are common in CAT scans
   (C) are fairly expensive to use
   (D) are necessary to the space program

5 According to the passage, which of the following is NOT true of the space program?

   (A) It only involves satellites.
   (B) It has made many technological advances.
   (C) It has benefited the lives of many people.
   (D) It has developed laser technology.

6 *Directions:* Complete the table below to summarize the information about the space program. Match the appropriate statements to the type of advance it applies to. *This question is worth 3 points.*

Statements

1. People can now use cellphones.
2. People have more knowledge of the stars.
3. Doctors can do laser surgery on people.
4. Regular people benefit from the space program.
5. Many people have cable television.
6. Some equipment does not need cords.
7. People can use body imaging now.

TYPES OF ADVANCES

Technological	Medical
•	•
•	•
•	

CHAPTER 04

Education
(Classification)

1. American Public and Private Schools
2. Friedrich Froebel
3. College Schools
4. Elite Universities
5. The First Western Universities
6. The TOEFL and TOEIC Exams
7. Homeschooling
8. Higher Education

CHAPTER 4 Education (Classification)

Understanding TOEFL Question Types & Reading Skills

1 Question Types — Rhetorical Purpose Questions

Rhetorical Purpose questions ask the reason why the author mentions certain information in the passage. These questions ask you to understand the function of a sentence or paragraph. Try to understand the logic in why the author mentions various facts or incidents.

- **Example Rhetorical Purpose Questions**
    - The author discusses "X" in paragraph 2 in order to ~
    - Why does the author mention "X"?
    - The author uses "X" as an example of ~

- **Useful Tips for Your Success**
    - Learn to
        → recognize important words and phrases.
        → understand the meanings of these words and phrases.
    - Think about
        → the connections between sentences.
        → the connections between paragraphs.

Sample Question

School Teaching Materials

Teachers use many kinds of materials in class. First, they have lots of standard materials. These are blackboards, printed handouts, and beam projectors. They also use online materials. These are materials such as websites, Internet newspapers, and online videos.

04-01

material [n] an object; a substance
standard [adj] regular; normal

Q Why does the author mention "printed handouts"?
  Ⓐ To compare them with websites
  Ⓑ To give an example of some standard materials
  Ⓒ To argue they are better than beam projectors
  Ⓓ To compare them with Internet newspapers

2 Reading Skills — Classification

Classification is organizing similar things or ideas into groups. People use classification to understand how two or more things or ideas relate to each other. When a writer uses classification, you should be able to notice the similarities in different things.

Check-Up

▶ The following are classified according to the passage. Choose one material to fill in the blank below.

Standard Materials	Online Materials
blackboards printed handouts _____	websites Internet newspapers online videos

Ⓐ chalk
Ⓑ pencils
Ⓒ movie screens
Ⓓ beam projectors

• **Exercise 1** •

American Public and Private Schools

04-02

America has many famous universities. Some of them are public schools. Governments support these schools. The University of North Carolina, the University of Texas, and UCLA are some prominent public schools. Others are private schools. A person, group, or organization owns these schools. Duke, Dartmouth, and Princeton are some famous private schools.

public adj free; supported by the government
prominent adj famous; well-known

Q The author uses "Duke, Dartmouth, and Princeton" as examples of _____
- Ⓐ famous public schools
- Ⓑ schools better than UCLA
- Ⓒ well-known private schools
- Ⓓ government-supported schools

Reading Skills **Classification**

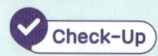 The following are classified according to the passage. Choose one university to fill in the blank below.

Famous Public Universities	Famous Private Universities
The University of North Carolina The University of Texas UCLA	_____ Dartmouth Princeton

- Ⓐ Duke
- Ⓑ Harvard
- Ⓒ Yale
- Ⓓ Stanford

• Exercise 2 •

Friedrich Froebel

04-03

In the past, most young children did not attend school. Instead, they stayed home and learned. One man wanted to alter this. His name was Friedrich Froebel. He created a school for young children. It would later be called kindergarten. He thought play was important for learning. He also believed that art, nature, and math were important. His ideas became popular. So many kindergartens opened in the 1800s.

attend v to go to a school, a class, an event, etc.
popular adj liked by many; well known

Q Why does the author mention "art, nature, and math" in the passage?

Ⓐ To call them the most important subjects
Ⓑ To argue that children do not need to learn them
Ⓒ To name some subjects appropriate when studying at home
Ⓓ To state that Froebel studied them very much

Reading Skills Classification

 **Check-Up** The following are classified according to the passage. Choose one activity to fill in the blank below.

Education before Froebel	Education after Froebel
no school for young children	play at school
────────────────	study art, nature, and math
no kindergartens	many kindergartens opened

Ⓐ studied with parents   Ⓑ worked in fields
Ⓒ had tutors at home   Ⓓ stayed home and learned

• **Exercise 3** •

College Schools

🎧 04-04

Many colleges have at least two different schools. These schools have various departments. Most of them have a school of liberal arts. Many others have a school of engineering. There are many majors in the liberal arts. These might be history, philosophy, and literature. Engineering schools have several majors, too. These include civil, chemical, and electrical engineering.

major n a course of study at a college or university
philosophy n the study of wisdom

Q The author uses "literature" as an example of

Ⓐ a kind of engineering
Ⓑ a liberal arts major
Ⓒ a major at an engineering school
Ⓓ a popular department at schools

Reading Skills Classification

 **Check-Up** The following are classified according to the passage. Choose one major to fill in the blank below.

Liberal Arts Majors	Engineering Majors
history philosophy literature	civil engineering –––––––––––––– electrical engineering

Ⓐ construction engineering   Ⓑ creative engineering
Ⓒ genetic engineering   Ⓓ chemical engineering

72

• **Exercise 4** •

Elite Universities

🎧 04-05

The United States has a lot of excellent universities. Many students dream of going to them. In the U.S., all of the Ivy League schools are superb. Four of them are Yale, Harvard, Cornell, and Columbia. There are many other great American schools. MIT, Stanford, Michigan, and UC Berkeley are all topnotch. They have brilliant professors and students.

superb adj excellent; outstanding; wonderful
topnotch adj superior; top quality

Q Why does the author mention "Cornell"?

Ⓐ To name an Ivy League university
Ⓑ To mention that most students dream of going there
Ⓒ To note that it has brilliant professors and students
Ⓓ To compare it with Harvard and Columbia

Reading Skills **Classification**

 The following are classified according to the passage. Choose one university to fill in the blank below.

Ivy League Schools	Great American Schools
Yale	MIT
Harvard	
Cornell	Michigan
Columbia	UC Berkeley

Ⓐ Tufts   Ⓑ Chicago   Ⓒ Stanford   Ⓓ Georgetown

Chapter ❹ 73

• **Exercise 5** •

The First Western Universities

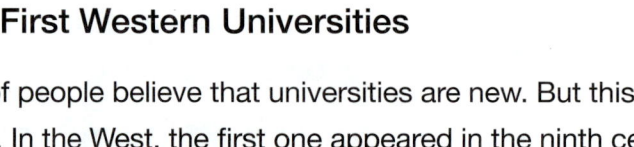

A lot of people believe that universities are new. But this is not true. In the West, the first one appeared in the ninth century. It was the University of Salerno. Salerno is a city in Italy. Later, one began in France. The University of Paris began in the twelfth century. The University of Oxford in England opened a short time later.

Early schools focused on religion. They taught subjects such as grammar, speech, and logic. This was the trivium. They also taught math, geometry, music, and astronomy. This was the quadrivium. These subjects prepared most students for life in the church. Over the years, many students went to these schools. Some of these schools still exist today.

focus v to emphasize; to stress
logic n reason; judgment

geometry n a field of mathematics

Q1 In paragraph 1, why does the author mention "the University of Salerno"?

Ⓐ To point out the first university in France
Ⓑ To talk about the West's first university
Ⓒ To compare it with the University of Oxford
Ⓓ To declare it the best university in the world

Q2 The author discusses "grammar" in paragraph 2 in order to

Ⓐ explain the hardest part of the quadrivium
Ⓑ state why most students learned religion
Ⓒ reveal why many students enjoyed learning
Ⓓ mention one of the parts of the trivium

Reading Skills Classification

 **Check-Up** The following are classified according to the passage. Choose one subject to fill in the blank below.

Trivium	Quadrivium
grammar	math
	geometry
logic	music
	astronomy

Ⓐ art Ⓑ history Ⓒ language Ⓓ speech

• **Exercise 6** •

The TOEFL and TOEIC Exams

Many students take standardized tests. They take them for various reasons. Some of these exams test English ability. Two of the major English exams are TOEFL and TOEIC.

Foreign students often take the TOEFL exam. They do this to get into American colleges. They need a high score to go to an American school. The TOEFL exam tests reading, listening, speaking, and writing abilities. Many people study very hard for this test.

Many other students take the TOEIC exam. This mostly covers business English. People applying to work at companies usually take this. It tests listening and reading skills. Students need to know English grammar, too. Students with good grades can get jobs at the best companies.

---

standardized **adj** identical; regular   score **n** a grade   cover **v** to go over; to include

Q1 In paragraph 2, why does the author mention "the TOEFL exam"?

Ⓐ To claim that it is a very hard test
Ⓑ To point out that that the test has four different parts
Ⓒ To argue that only students with the best scores can go to college
Ⓓ To state that foreign students take it to go to American colleges

Q2 The author discusses "the TOEIC exam" in paragraph 3 in order to

Ⓐ describe what it tests
Ⓑ explain how people get good jobs
Ⓒ note why students should study grammar
Ⓓ state that only foreigners take this test

Reading Skills **Classification**

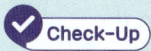 **Check-Up** The following are classified according to the passage. Choose one ability to fill in the blank below.

TOEFL Exam	TOEIC Exam
reading listening speaking	reading listening English grammar

Ⓐ writing   Ⓑ English grammar   Ⓒ business English   Ⓓ communication skills

• Exercise 7 •

Homeschooling

🎧 04-08

Nowadays, many American children do not attend school. Instead, they stay home. They do homeschooling. They take all of their classes at home. One of their parents may be their instructor. Many homeschooled students do very well. They often even go to the best colleges.

Students do homeschooling for many reasons. Sometimes their parents just want to educate their own children. But many times they do homeschooling to learn different subjects. Public schools often teach English, history, math, and science. They might also teach art and music. But those are the only subjects. However, homeschooling students can learn many more subjects at home. They can study religion. They might learn philosophy, too. They can also learn many different languages.

attend v to go to   instructor n a teacher; a tutor   educate v to teach; to instruct

Q1 The author discusses "parents" in paragraph 1 in order to
- Ⓐ explain why children stay home
- Ⓑ mention why homeschooling is successful
- Ⓒ describe why some students go to good colleges
- Ⓓ state who homeschooled students' teachers may be

Q2 In paragraph 2, the author uses "philosophy" as an example of
- Ⓐ a difficult subject
- Ⓑ a homeschooling subject
- Ⓒ a public school subject
- Ⓓ a private school subject

Reading Skills Classification

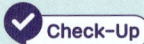 **The following are classified according to the passage. Choose one subject to fill in the blank below.**

Public School Subjects	Homeschooling Subjects
English history math science	all public school subjects _____ philosophy languages

Ⓐ religion   Ⓑ science   Ⓒ Spanish   Ⓓ social studies

• Exercise 8 •

Higher Education

After high school, many students continue to go to school. They can do their studies in two different ways. First, there is traditional higher education. And next is alternative higher education.

Traditionally, many students go to public or private colleges. They may also enroll at community colleges. Or some of them may decide to go to junior colleges. Students at junior colleges only study for two years.

But these days, alternative education is getting popular. So some students do distance learning. They study at their homes, not in classrooms. Others go to cyber universities. They do all of their work over the Internet. And other people just attend private academies. So people have many learning options now.

traditional adj usual; conventional
alternative adj substitute
enroll v to register; to sign up for

Q1 The author discusses "junior colleges" in paragraph 2 in order to
- Ⓐ claim students there only study for two years
- Ⓑ mention one form of traditional education
- Ⓒ contrast them with public and private colleges
- Ⓓ argue that they are better than community colleges

Q2 In paragraph 3, why does the author mention "alternative education"?
- Ⓐ To compare it to higher education
- Ⓑ To argue that all students should try it
- Ⓒ To explain how people use the Internet to study
- Ⓓ To show some higher education options

Reading Skills Classification

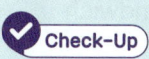 The following are classified according to the passage. Choose one type of education to fill in the blank below.

Traditional Higher Education	Alternative Higher Education
public or private college community college junior college	_____ cyber university private academy

- Ⓐ private tutoring
- Ⓑ graduate school
- Ⓒ distance learning
- Ⓓ on-the-job training

Grammar Point

Articles

Times to Use Indefinite Articles	Indefinite Articles
a (before a consonant) **an** (before a vowel or a vowel sound)	• a week / a dog / a classroom / a river / a student • an hour / an umbrella / an answer / an onion / an eagle
the same	• Birds of a feather flock together. • The people of a country are its citizens.
one	• I have a brother and two sisters. • There is a man at the door.
certain	• Please pass me a spoon. • I'd like to get an A in this class.
divisions of time	• I write to her twice a month. • They exercise three times a week.
useful expressions	• I'll have a look at that paper now. • She made a visit to our house. • The cat made a strange noise. • Steve made a speech yesterday. • Go faster. I'm in a hurry. • The story finally came to an end. • Keep an eye on my wallet, please.

Times to Use Definite Articles	Definite Articles
a specific person or thing	• Open the door. • Look at the blackboard. • May I go to the bathroom?
before natural things	• the sun / the Earth / the sky / the moon / the sea
defined by a prepositional phrase	• the road to Busan / the answer to the question
when talking about the same noun again	• I had a sandwich and an apple for lunch. The sandwich wasn't very good, but the apple was nice.
before instruments	• play the piano / play the drums / play the violin
before ordinal numbers	• the first page / the second man / the third puppy
before superlatives	• the most interesting movie / the strongest person
with proper nouns	• the Han River / the Atlantic Ocean / the Alps / the White House

Grammar Check-Up

A Circle the best answer choices. There can be two options.

1 David gave (a / an / the / ¢) umbrella to Mary since it was raining.
2 (A / An / The / ¢) answer to the question is forty-two.
3 Many crocodiles live in (a / an / the / ¢) Nile River.
4 Do you have (a / an / the / ¢) picture of yourself when you were young?
5 He always drinks a glass of (a / an / the / ¢) milk at dinner.

B Write *a*, *an*, *the*, or "zero" ¢ in the blanks.

1 We are taking _____ trip to India this summer.
2 I talked to _____ Stephanie about our homework assignment.
3 Send me _____ email as soon as you can.
4 Jason just called you on _____ telephone.
5 When are you coming _____ home this evening?

C Read the following story and fill in the blanks with articles.

Every morning, Jason wakes up and takes _____ shower. Then, he gets dressed and goes to _____ kitchen for breakfast. He usually eats some bacon and drinks _____ glass of orange juice. After breakfast, he puts his books in his bag and goes to school. _____ school bus picks him up at 7:30 in _____ morning. Jason has _____ lot of friends at school, so he really loves going there. The first thing he does is talk to his friends. Sometimes they chat for over _____ hour! They talk about many different things before _____ school bell rings. After that, it is time for class.

Vocabulary Review

A Circle the words that best complete the sentences.

1 Many (foreign / traditional) students take the TOEFL exam.
2 Albert Einstein had one of the most (standardized / brilliant) minds in history.
3 A (junior / private) college is a two-year school.
4 The teacher gave the printed (handouts / videos) to the students.
5 The (government / university) is holding elections for mayor this week.

B Choose the best words to complete the sentences.

1 The test will _____ all the material the students learned last month.

   A get
   B continue
   C cover
   D begin

2 Schools must teach their students many different _____.

   A majors
   B reasons
   C subjects
   D tests

3 Nowadays, there are many _____ materials such as websites.

   A online
   B traditional
   C standard
   D private

4 Nancy was the most _____ student at the entire school.

   A foreign
   B various
   C alternative
   D popular

5 _____ is a branch of mathematics.

   A Speech
   B Logic
   C Geometry
   D Philosophy

C Choose the words with the closest meanings to the highlighted words.

1. Brad is a topnotch employee at the company.
   - Ⓐ higher
   - Ⓑ different
   - Ⓒ superb
   - Ⓓ popular

2. Mr. Patterson did a good job of teaching the students at school.
   - Ⓐ educating
   - Ⓑ learning
   - Ⓒ attending
   - Ⓓ taking

3. George Washington is a very prominent person in American history.
   - Ⓐ brilliant
   - Ⓑ superb
   - Ⓒ public
   - Ⓓ famous

4. Sally got the highest score in the class on her math test.
   - Ⓐ option
   - Ⓑ grade
   - Ⓒ education
   - Ⓓ exam

5. You must alter this report because it has some mistakes.
   - Ⓐ change
   - Ⓑ delete
   - Ⓒ call
   - Ⓓ attend

D Complete the sentences by filling in the blanks with the best words from the list. Change the forms of the words if necessary. Use each word only once.

| homeschooling | focus | blackboard | support | liberal |

1. Eric is studying the _____ arts instead of engineering.
2. Mrs. Richardson writes everything on the _____ during class.
3. You need to _____ on the question to think of the answer.
4. Many parents like _____ because they can teach their children more subjects.
5. I will _____ you as you try to become a doctor.

Practice Test

Lecture and Discussion Classes

Teachers have a wide variety of styles. Yet most classes can be categorized into two types. They are lecture and discussion classes. Lecture classes mostly involve the teacher speaking. Discussion classes have a lot of student participation.

Lecture classes are more common. In these classes, the teacher speaks most of the time. The students listen and take notes. These classes let students learn a great deal. This method is ideal for topics such as history, math, and science. Many times, teachers permit questions from students. But they do not encourage student participation. They instead focus on giving as much as information to the students.

Discussion classes often involve lecturing. Yet teachers also encourage their students to participate. They let students ask questions. They also encourage students to provide their own opinions. In many cases, teachers organize group discussions. These allow students to talk with one another. English and social studies classes may be of this type.

Both styles are effective. And students can learn from them. But most students prefer one to the other.

---

participation *n* the act of taking part in an action
encourage *v* to promote or advance

1   In paragraph 1, the author implies that teachers
    - (A) should let students talk in class
    - (B) must study hard to get their jobs
    - (C) prefer lectures to discussions
    - (D) do not all teach the same way

2   The word "permit" in the passage is closest in meaning to
    - (A) ban
    - (B) suggest
    - (C) allow
    - (D) approve

3   In paragraph 2, all of the following questions are answered EXCEPT:
    - (A) What classes often involve teachers lecturing?
    - (B) What do students usually do in lecture classes?
    - (C) How much should students learn in lecture classes?
    - (D) What is the main objective of teachers in lecture classes?

4   The word "These" in the passage refers to
    - (A) Their own opinions
    - (B) Many cases
    - (C) Teachers
    - (D) Group discussions

5   According to paragraph 3, which of the following is true of discussion classes?
    - (A) Students learn more in them than in lecture classes.
    - (B) Teachers sometimes lecture in them.
    - (C) They are good for science and math classes.
    - (D) Students sometimes give presentations in them.

6 *Directions:* Complete the table below to summarize the information about classes. Match the appropriate statements to the type of class it applies to. *This question is worth 3 points.*

Statements

1. Often features in math and history classes
2. May involve students dividing into groups
3. Requires students to listen and to take notes
4. Teaches students how to think for themselves
5. Gives much information to students
6. Allows students to give their own thoughts
7. Lets students learn about reading comprehension

TYPE OF CLASS

Lecture	Discussion
•	•
•	•
•	

CHAPTER 05

Economics
(Guessing Unknown Words)

1. Taxes
2. Adam Smith
3. Money
4. Loans
5. Recessions and Depressions
6. Economic Systems
7. Stocks
8. Supply and Demand

CHAPTER 5 Economics (Guessing Unknown Words)

Understanding TOEFL Question Types & Reading Skills

1 Question Types — Vocabulary Questions

Vocabulary questions ask you to determine the meanings of words or phrases in the passage. Many times, a word may have several meanings. The meaning depends upon how the writer uses the word in the passage. Try to recognize how the writer is using a word or phrase. Then you will be able to answer the question correctly.

- **Example Vocabulary Questions**
  - ▸ The word "X" in the passage is closest in meaning to ~
  - ▸ In stating "X", the author means that ~

- **Useful Tips for Your Success**

  ▸ Remember that → one word may have many different meanings.

  → you should be able to substitute the new word into the passage.

  ▸ Don't → simply choose a word's most common meaning.

  → choose an answer just because it looks right.

Sample Question

Bartering

Nowadays, people use money. But once there was no money. So people bartered. This is trading one thing for another. People decided on their items' values. Perhaps a farmer traded ten tomatoes for two pairs of shoes. Or a fisherman traded one fish for three apples.

🎧 05-01

decide *v* to choose; to determine
perhaps *adv* possibly; maybe

Q The word "values" in the passage is closest in meaning to

Ⓐ abilities
Ⓑ worth
Ⓒ standards
Ⓓ appearances

2 Reading Skills — Guessing Unknown Words

Guessing unknown words is determining the meaning of a word from the context of the passage. Many times, you can guess the meaning of a word by looking at the other words in the same sentence or a sentence next to it. Look at these words carefully, and you should be able to guess the unknown word's meaning.

Check-Up

▶ Guess the meaning of the underlined word.

So people <u>bartered</u>. This is trading one thing for another.

Ⓐ sold
Ⓑ purchased
Ⓒ manufactured
Ⓓ exchanged

• Exercise 1 •

Taxes

 05-02

All governments require money. Without money, they cannot provide various services. So they need to raise money. One way to acquire it is through taxes. The most common ones are income and sales taxes. However, there are many more. People must pay property taxes on their homes. There are also import taxes on goods from other countries.

require v to need
property n a possession; a belonging

Q The word "common" in the passage is closest in meaning to

Ⓐ rare
Ⓑ usual
Ⓒ expensive
Ⓓ famous

Reading Skills Guessing Unknown Words

 **Check-Up** Guess the meaning of the underlined word.

So they need to raise money. One way to acquire it is through taxes.

Ⓐ spend
Ⓑ loan
Ⓒ make
Ⓓ get

• **Exercise 2** •

Adam Smith

05-03

Adam Smith lived from 1723 to 1790. He was one of the world's most important economists. He wrote the book *The Wealth of Nations*. In his manuscript, he proposed his theory of free market economics. In it, the government does not interfere in the market. Instead, people can do whatever they want. They also try to make as much money as possible.

economist n a person who studies economics
interfere v to obstruct; to hinder

Q The word "theory" in the passage is closest in meaning to
Ⓐ idea
Ⓑ promise
Ⓒ support
Ⓓ request

Reading Skills Guessing Unknown Words

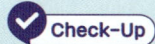 Guess the meaning of the underlined word.

He wrote the book *The Wealth of Nations*. In his manuscript, he proposed his theory of free market economics.
Ⓐ study
Ⓑ book
Ⓒ paper
Ⓓ report

• **Exercise 3** •

Money

05-04

There are many different kinds of money. First, people often use coins and paper money. They spend this as cash. In addition, they can utilize other kinds of currency. For example, some people pay with checks. With a check, the bank will withdraw money from a person's checking account. Others prefer to use credit cards as money.

cash n money
checking account n a bank account

Q The word "withdraw" in the passage is closest in meaning to

- Ⓐ insert
- Ⓑ include
- Ⓒ credit
- Ⓓ take out

Reading Skills Guessing Unknown Words

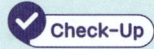 Guess the meaning of the underlined word.

They spend this as cash. In addition, they can utilize other kinds of <u>currency</u>.

- Ⓐ money
- Ⓑ checks
- Ⓒ credit
- Ⓓ gold

• **Exercise 4** •

Loans

When people need money, they may acquire a loan from a bank. A loan provides a person with money to use in various ways. Some of these include purchasing a house or a vehicle or running a business. There are terms to a loan that a borrower must abide by. The loan is paid back in installments. It is usually made monthly. In addition, interest on the loan must be paid.

purchase v to buy
run v to operate; to be in control of

Q The phrase "abide by" in the passage is closest in meaning to
Ⓐ remember
Ⓑ approach
Ⓒ follow
Ⓓ negotiate

Reading Skills Guessing Unknown Words

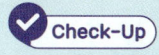 Guess the meaning of the underlined word.

The loan is paid back in installments. It is usually made monthly.
Ⓐ full
Ⓑ haste
Ⓒ appearance
Ⓓ portions

• **Exercise 5** •

Recessions and Depressions

Most countries' economies improve over time. This often happens very slowly. Still, economies almost always get better. However, a country's economy may become bad at times. People may lose their jobs. They start to make less money. Companies lose money and go bankrupt, too. This may even occur for several months. After six months of negative growth, people can call this time a recession.

Recessions can last for a long time. They can also sometimes get even worse. People call this a depression. A depression is a severe recession.

The Great Depression started in the United States in 1929. It lasted for over ten years until World War II began. It was very harmful to the American economy.

improve v to get better
occur v to happen
negative adj harmful; not positive

Q1 The word "growth" in the passage is closest in meaning to
- Ⓐ aging
- Ⓑ profit
- Ⓒ expansion
- Ⓓ size

Q2 The word "severe" in the passage is closest in meaning to
- Ⓐ dangerous
- Ⓑ unique
- Ⓒ harmless
- Ⓓ harsh

Reading Skills   Guessing Unknown Words

 Guess the meaning of the underlined word.

Companies lose money and go bankrupt, too.
- Ⓐ profitable
- Ⓑ broke
- Ⓒ smaller
- Ⓓ better

• **Exercise 6** •

Economic Systems

There are many kinds of economic systems. Most countries practice capitalism. This is a system of private ownership. For the most part, people own and operate businesses for profit. They want to make as much money as they can. In capitalism, the government attempts not to interfere with the economy. It will generally not bother private citizens. It will let them run the economy. However, it will occasionally pass some business laws.

This is not true in socialism. Under socialism, the government owns most businesses. There is less of a focus on making a profit. Instead, people think more about the well-being of the community. In socialism, governments often nationalize various industries. This means the government takes the industries over and runs them.

kind n a type; a sort
community n a society; a neighborhood; a region
nationalize v to take over for the government

Q1 The word "practice" in the passage is closest in meaning to
- Ⓐ follow
- Ⓑ rehearse
- Ⓒ provide
- Ⓓ play

Q2 The word "attempts" in the passage is closest in meaning to
- Ⓐ tries
- Ⓑ thinks
- Ⓒ considers
- Ⓓ wishes

Reading Skills Guessing Unknown Words

Check-Up Guess the meaning of the underlined word.

In capitalism, the government attempts not to interfere with the economy. It will generally not bother private citizens.
- Ⓐ hurt
- Ⓑ disturb
- Ⓒ strengthen
- Ⓓ misuse

• Exercise 7 •

Stocks

05-08

Many companies are private. So only one person or a group of people owns them. However, there are some businesses called corporations. Many people can own a corporation. Corporations issue stocks. A stock is a share in a company. Corporations generally release millions of shares. This way, thousands of different people can be part owners of one company.

People can buy and sell shares of stock. They often do this on stock markets. The most renowned stock market is the New York Stock Exchange in the United States. Every day, people trade millions of shares of stocks. The price of stocks goes up and down all the time. People always try to buy low and sell high.

private adj owned by an individual or group of individuals
corporation n a company that issues stock
stock market n a place for the buying and selling of stocks

Q1 The word "generally" in the passage is closest in meaning to
Ⓐ always
Ⓑ sometimes
Ⓒ usually
Ⓓ rarely

Q2 The word "renowned" in the passage is closest in meaning to
Ⓐ wealthy
Ⓑ famous
Ⓒ respected
Ⓓ exceptional

| Reading Skills | Guessing Unknown Words |

 **Guess the meaning of the underlined word.**

Corporations issue stocks. A stock is a share in a company.
Ⓐ print
Ⓑ purchase
Ⓒ release
Ⓓ save

• **Exercise 8** •

Supply and Demand

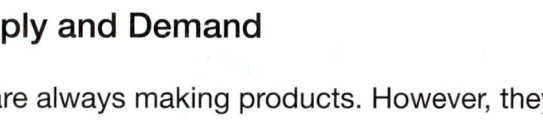
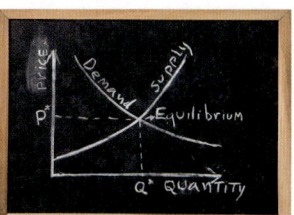

Companies are always making products. However, they make various amounts of different products. The amount of products available is the supply. This is always a definite number. People usually want to buy certain products. Of course, some products are more popular than others. The rate people want a certain product is the demand. This is more difficult to calculate. So economists always try to determine it.

Both supply and demand always affect the price. Sometimes supply is high while demand is low. Then the price will be low, too. However, perhaps demand is high while supply is low. Then the price will be high. Stores always use supply and demand to establish the prices of their products.

supply n the amount of a product available
demand n how much people want a product
various adj different; diverse

Q1 The word "definite" in the passage is closest in meaning to
- Ⓐ random
- Ⓑ same
- Ⓒ possible
- Ⓓ exact

Q2 The word "establish" in the passage is closest in meaning to
- Ⓐ ask
- Ⓑ set
- Ⓒ change
- Ⓓ lower

Reading Skills Guessing Unknown Words

 **Check-Up** Guess the meaning of the underlined word.

The rate people want a certain product is the demand. This is more difficult to calculate.
- Ⓐ add
- Ⓑ understand
- Ⓒ determine
- Ⓓ subtract

Grammar Point

Adverbs

▮ **Conjunctions** are adverbs such as *however*, *yet*, and *though*.

Functions	Conjunctions	Example Sentences
Appositive	for example that is in other words	• David enjoys movies. For example, he sees one every weekend. • He is crazy about soccer. That is, he wants to be a pro. • He never studies. In other words, he does not like school.
Concessive	however still nevertheless nonetheless yet only though	• She enjoys traveling; however, she hates airplanes. • Adam is not very big. Still, he wants to play football. • She caught a bad cold. Nevertheless, she went to school. • They disliked each other. Nonetheless, they agreed. • He enjoys amusement parks, yet he hates roller coasters. • She wanted to leave. Only her mom told her to stay. • Though he ran very hard, he lost the race.
Inferential	otherwise else then in that case	• She should wear a sweater. Otherwise, she will be cold. • Be careful, or else you will make a big mess. • If you like swimming, then you should go to the beach. • He did not come. In that case, I will give you a ride.
Resultive	therefore so hence of course consequently accordingly	• He hates shopping; therefore, he never goes to the mall. • We love baseball, so we play every weekend. • I study hard; hence, I get good grades. • He has a new sports car. Of course, it was expensive. • She slept until noon; consequently, she was late for class. • A man stole her car; accordingly, she told the police.
Additive	besides also moreover likewise in addition	• I went to bed early. Besides, I had a test the next morning. • That is a nice bag. It is also very large. • The game was boring. Moreover, it was too long. • John is married. He is likewise a father. • We visited Japan. In addition, we went to China.

Grammar Check-Up

A Choose the conjunctions that best complete the sentences.

1 We are leaving school at once. (However / Consequently), we will get home early.

2 You need to be careful. (Otherwise / Likewise) you will get in trouble.

3 Jane is a great student. (For example / In that case), she studies every day.

4 The game ended, (moreover / yet) they did not leave the ballpark.

5 If Eric works hard, (then / so) he will finish his project on time.

B Choose the correct words for each blank.

1 You are being too loud. _____, you need to be more polite.
   ⓐ Otherwise   ⓑ Of course   ⓒ Moreover   ⓓ Though

2 I did not study for the test. _____, I got an A⁺ on the exam.
   ⓐ Nonetheless   ⓑ Therefore   ⓒ Else   ⓓ Accordingly

3 _____ Mary got a new job, she did not make a lot of money.
   ⓐ Consequently   ⓑ In that case   ⓒ Still   ⓓ Though

4 I may not meet you at the airport. _____, I will send Mr. Smith instead.
   ⓐ In that case   ⓑ Besides   ⓒ Likewise   ⓓ For example

5 Kevin is going to the store. He is _____ going to visit his friends.
   ⓐ therefore   ⓑ also   ⓒ hence   ⓓ that is

C Read the following story and fill in the blanks with the conjunctions in the box.

> in addition   in other words   therefore   likewise   nevertheless   then   so

School began early in the morning for Sally. _____, she woke up very early. _____, she had to get up at seven. She was not very happy about that. _____, she got up and ate breakfast. _____, she got dressed and went to school. She had a test that day. She did not study for it. Still, she did very well on it. _____, she got the highest grade in the class. Sally was very happy about this. _____ she and her friends bought some ice cream after school. Finally, she went home around five o'clock. _____, her friends went home, too.

Vocabulary Review

A Circle the words that best complete the sentences.

1 John studies (economist / economics) at his school.
2 People always want the unemployment (rate / loan) to be low.
3 You can buy and sell stocks on the stock (market / share).
4 The United States suffered through the Great (Recession / Depression) in the 1930s.
5 A person with no money is (bankrupt / renowned).

B Choose the best words to complete the sentences.

1 Kevin went to the bank to _____ some money.
   A deal
   B withdraw
   C issue
   D focus

2 They _____ for some food since they had no money.
   A bartered
   B wrote
   C proposed
   D happened

3 Many people do not like paying high _____ to the government.
   A supplies
   B rates
   C economies
   D taxes

4 Private ownership is an important part of _____.
   A recession
   B capitalism
   C economist
   D socialism

5 The _____ rate on the loan she got is very high.
   A supply
   B system
   C interest
   D capitalist

C Choose the words with the closest meanings to the highlighted words.

1. We are all hoping that the economy will get better soon.
   - Ⓐ affect
   - Ⓑ improve
   - Ⓒ utilize
   - Ⓓ withdraw

2. The government took over several failing companies last week.
   - Ⓐ accounted
   - Ⓑ marketed
   - Ⓒ demanded
   - Ⓓ nationalized

3. I do not have that much money to spend today.
   - Ⓐ credit
   - Ⓑ coin
   - Ⓒ cash
   - Ⓓ check

4. He hopes to acquire a new job soon.
   - Ⓐ obtain
   - Ⓑ apply for
   - Ⓒ learn about
   - Ⓓ research

5. Mr. Williams needs some help right now.
   - Ⓐ demands
   - Ⓑ occurs
   - Ⓒ requires
   - Ⓓ interferes

D Complete the sentences by filling in the blanks with the best words from the list. Change the forms of the words if necessary. Use each word only once.

> available   economist   checking   supply   private

1. Jason opened a(n) _____ account at his local bank.
2. There are no seats currently _____ on that flight.
3. A(n) _____ citizen is the owner of that company.
4. The demand for fish this month exceeds the _____.
5. Larry wanted to become a(n) _____ after graduating from college.

Practice Test

Different Types of Money in History

05-10

Today, there are many types of money. For example, people can pay for goods and services with cash, credit cards, or checks. They can even use cryptocurrency like Bitcoin. These are not the only types of money people have used though. Throughout history, there have been other kinds of money.

Around 1,200 B.C., some people used seashells as money. The Romans often paid soldiers with salt. People in the past also used cattle, leather, stones, and tobacco as money. Metal was first used as money around 2,000 B.C. This was in Babylon. However, the first metal coins appeared in Lydia. This was in the seventh century B.C. They were made of electrum.

The use of coins spread fast. People made coins with copper, silver, gold, and other metals. Later, the Chinese created money from paper. They did this around 1,000 A.D. Over time, coins and paper currency became common everywhere. People still use them today even though there are other types of money.

cryptocurrency n a modern electronic form of money
electrum n an alloy made of gold and silver

1 According to paragraph 1, which of the following is true of money?

   Ⓐ It only consists of cash, credit cards, and checks.
   Ⓑ People can receive it for work they do.
   Ⓒ Types of it have changed over time.
   Ⓓ Its value is not always the same.

2 In paragraph 2, the author uses "salt" as an example of

   Ⓐ money used in Babylon
   Ⓑ a type of money in the past
   Ⓒ a material people made coins with
   Ⓓ a payment method in Lydia

3 The word "They" in the passage refers to

   Ⓐ The Romans
   Ⓑ People in the past
   Ⓒ Cattle, leather, stones, and tobacco
   Ⓓ The first metal coins

4 The word "currency" in the passage is closest in meaning to

   Ⓐ money
   Ⓑ checks
   Ⓒ bonds
   Ⓓ stocks

5 In paragraph 3, all of the following questions are answered EXCEPT:

   Ⓐ Why did people stop using coins?
   Ⓑ What metals were coins made of in the past?
   Ⓒ When was the paper money created?
   Ⓓ Who made the first paper money?

6 *Directions:* An introductory sentence for a brief summary of the passage is provided below. Complete the summary by selecting the THREE answer choices that express the most important ideas in the passage. Some answer choices do not belong in the summary because they express ideas that are not presented in the passage or are minor ideas in the passage. *This question is worth 2 points.*

People have used various types of money for thousands of years.

-
-
-

Answer Choices

1. People can earn money by doing different jobs.
2. Coins and paper money were invented in the past.
3. Bitcoin is a popular type of money today.
4. People use money to pay for goods and services.
5. There are various kinds of money today.
6. Some people used seashells or salt as money.

CHAPTER 06

Sociology
(Mapping)

1. Divorce
2. Sports Organizations
3. Public Transportation
4. Social Media
5. The Suburbs
6. Gated Communities
7. Single-Parent Homes
8. Peer Pressure

CHAPTER 6 Sociology (Mapping)

Understanding TOEFL Question Types & Reading Skills

1 Question Types — Reference Questions

Reference questions ask you to recognize how some words refer to others in the passage. These questions usually ask about a pronoun and the word or words it refers to. Sometimes the questions ask about other words such as *which*, *that*, or *this*. The answer choices are always a word or words from the passage.

- **Example Reference Questions**
  ▶ The word "X" in the passage refers to ~

- **Useful Tips for Your Success**
  ▶ Make sure
   → you don't confuse feminine and masculine pronouns.
   → you can substitute the answer choice for the pronoun.

  ▶ Don't
   → match a singular pronoun with a plural answer.
   → match a plural pronoun with a singular answer.

Sample Question

Volunteering

Many people often participate in charity work. They volunteer to work somewhere. They may go to hospitals, libraries, or homeless shelters. They go to those places. Then they often work for a few hours. And they do not even receive any money.

volunteer v to work for free; to choose to do something
charity n assistance; aid

Q The word "They" in the passage refers to
- Ⓐ People
- Ⓑ Hospitals
- Ⓒ Libraries
- Ⓓ Homeless shelters

2 Reading Skills — Mapping

Mapping is a way to organize information. You draw diagrams to show how all of the ideas in a paragraph or passage relate to one another. When you do this, you can easily notice the connection of one idea to another.

Check-Up

▶ What is the best answer for the blank below?

```
Many people ── Volunteering ── • hospitals
                             • libraries
                             • homeless shelters
                             │
                         • work for a few _____
                         • do not make any money
```

- Ⓐ minutes
- Ⓑ hours
- Ⓒ days
- Ⓓ weeks

• **Exercise 1** •

Divorce

06-02

Sometimes a married couple has many issues. They usually fight over money and property. They sometimes even argue about their children. They may try to solve their problems. But they often cannot. In that case, they get divorced. A divorce legally ends a couple's marriage. This can create many problems though. This can especially harm their children for a long time.

legally adv officially; lawfully
harm v to hurt; to injure

Q The word "This" in the passage refers to

Ⓐ A married couple
Ⓑ Money
Ⓒ Property
Ⓓ A divorce

Reading Skills Mapping

✓ **Check-Up** What is the best answer for the blank below?

A married couple
- fight over money & property
- argue about their children
Try to solve their problems

- creates many _____
- can harm their children for a long time

Divorce

Fail to solve their problems

Ⓐ problems　　Ⓑ property　　Ⓒ money　　Ⓓ children

106

• **Exercise 2** •

Sports Organizations

🎧 06-03

Many American adults and children participate in sports leagues. Cities and counties operate them. They usually run soccer, baseball, basketball, and football leagues. These let people get exercise and play team sports. And they help children learn about teamwork and make good friends. These leagues are often cheap. The teams typically play on weekends or in the evenings.

participate in [phr] to take part in
county [n] a region; an area; a district

Q The word "they" in the passage refers to
Ⓐ many American adults and children
Ⓑ cities and counties
Ⓒ sports leagues
Ⓓ children

Reading Skills Mapping

Check-Up What is the best answer for the blank below?

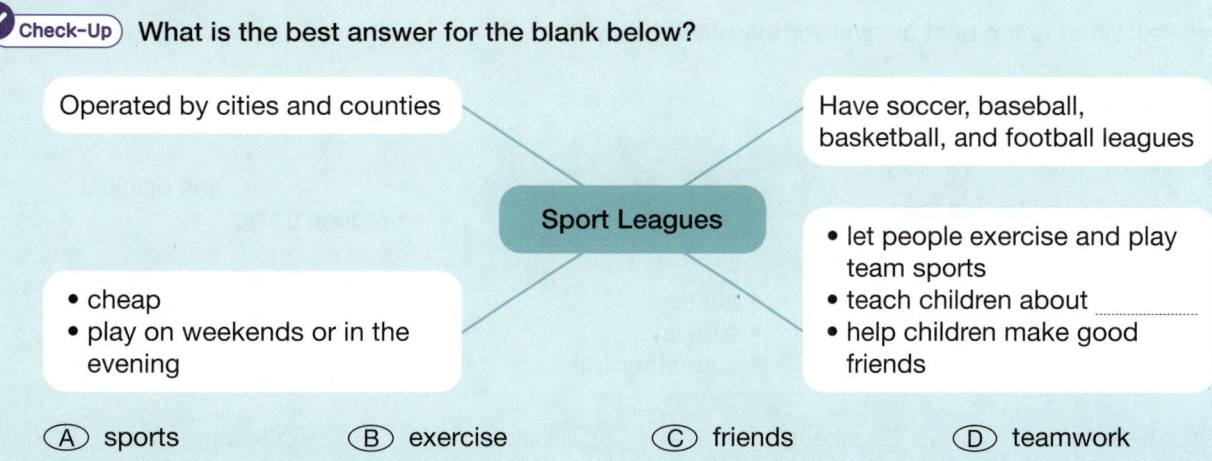

Ⓐ sports   Ⓑ exercise   Ⓒ friends   Ⓓ teamwork

• **Exercise 3** •

Public Transportation

06-04

People in many cities do not have their own cars. Personal vehicles are too expensive. There is also not enough space for them in cities. So most cities have public transportation systems. These are systems such as buses, subways, and commuter trains. They provide their citizens with cheap and efficient transportation. They also help reduce traffic.

commuter train [n] a train that goes from the suburbs to downtown
efficient [adj] well-organized; effective

Q The word "them" in the passage refers to
  Ⓐ people
  Ⓑ many cities
  Ⓒ personal vehicles
  Ⓓ public transportation systems

Reading Skills Mapping

Check-Up What is the best answer for the blank below?

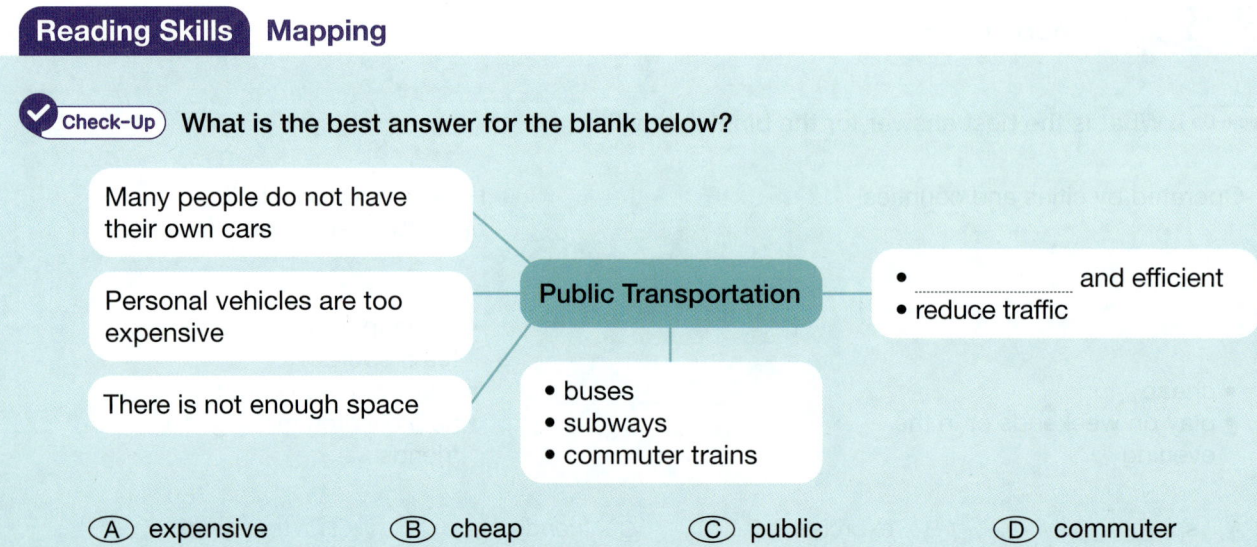

Ⓐ expensive   Ⓑ cheap   Ⓒ public   Ⓓ commuter

Exercise 4

Social Media

Social media provides young people with a great amount of entertainment. However, it also comes with a large number of drawbacks. Some young people are addicted to social media. They spend several hours each day using it. As a result, they ignore their schoolwork. They do not exercise enough or play sports either. Some of them also have trouble interacting with other people their age.

drawback n a disadvantage; something that harms instead of helping
interact v to communicate with others

Q The word "them" in the passage refers to
- Ⓐ young people
- Ⓑ several hours
- Ⓒ sports
- Ⓓ other people

Reading Skills Mapping

Check-Up What is the best answer for the blank below?

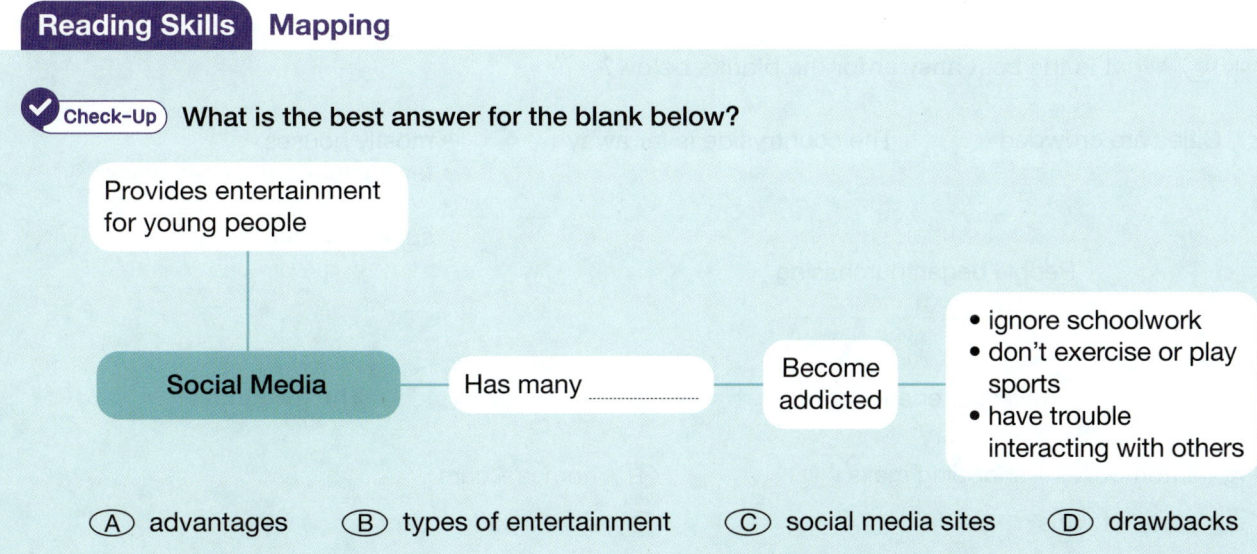

- Ⓐ advantages
- Ⓑ types of entertainment
- Ⓒ social media sites
- Ⓓ drawbacks

• **Exercise 5** •

The Suburbs

06-06

For the longest time, people lived either in the country or the city. However, the countryside was far away from everything. Cities were usually too crowded as well. Then, in the 1900s, people began purchasing automobiles. Now they could travel faster and farther. So people began leaving the cities. But they did not move to the countryside. Instead, they moved to the suburbs.

Suburbs are like towns near the city. They mostly have houses. There are typically few factories or companies there. Suburbs may have shopping malls and supermarkets. They are much better places to live in than cities. People often work in cities. But they live in suburbs. Thanks to cars, they can do this.

suburb n a small city or town outside a large city   **factory** n a building where people make things
countryside n the country

Q1 The word "they" in the passage refers to
- Ⓐ cities
- Ⓑ automobiles
- Ⓒ people
- Ⓓ suburbs

Q2 The word "there" in the passage refers to
- Ⓐ suburbs
- Ⓑ houses
- Ⓒ factories
- Ⓓ companies

Reading Skills Mapping

Check-Up What is the best answer for the blanks below?

- Ⓐ automobiles – shopping malls
- Ⓑ homes – cars
- Ⓒ cities – towns
- Ⓓ countryside – cars

• Exercise 6 •

Gated Communities

Some places in the world are getting dangerous. So many people are choosing to live in gated communities. These are like small cities. A large fence surrounds the entire complex. People must pass through gates to get in and out of it. Many times, guards protect these communities.

There are many things inside these communities. People's homes are there. There are also often shopping centers and supermarkets. There are sometimes even schools in them. In many of these places, people do not have to go outside of their community very often. These places are becoming popular in America. But other countries, including China and South Africa, are also building them these days.

gated adj fenced in; having a fence
complex n a large area
build v to construct; to make

Q1 The word "it" in the passage refers to
- Ⓐ the world
- Ⓑ small cities
- Ⓒ a large fence
- Ⓓ the entire complex

Q2 The word "them" in the passage refers to
- Ⓐ these communities
- Ⓑ people's homes
- Ⓒ shopping centers
- Ⓓ supermarkets

Reading Skills Mapping

Check-Up What is the best answer for the blanks below?

Some places are getting _____①_____

- A large fence surrounds the entire complex
- Guards protect these communities

Developed in America, China & South Africa

Gated Communities

- people's homes
- shopping centers & supermarkets
- _____②_____

- Ⓐ gated – places
- Ⓑ popular – communities
- Ⓒ dangerous – schools
- Ⓓ shopping – countries

• **Exercise 7** •

Single-Parent Homes

06-08

For the past few decades, more and more Americans have been getting divorced. Sadly, these couples often have children. So they have to grow up with only one parent in the house. Sociologists call these single-parent homes.

Children from single-parent homes often have difficult times. They usually miss either their mother or father. They might not perform as well as other students at school. And they sometimes have emotional problems. These can cause big problems later in life. Most researchers believe it is better to grow up with both parents. However, this is not possible for many children. So the parent they live with must try very hard to raise them properly.

decade n a period of ten years
sociologist n a person who studies society
perform v to do; to carry out; to achieve

Q1 The word "they" in the passage refers to
  Ⓐ the past few decades
  Ⓑ more and more Americans
  Ⓒ these couples
  Ⓓ children

Q2 The word "These" in the passage refers to
  Ⓐ Children
  Ⓑ Other students
  Ⓒ Single-parent homes
  Ⓓ Emotional problems

Reading Skills **Mapping**

 What is the best answer for the blanks below?

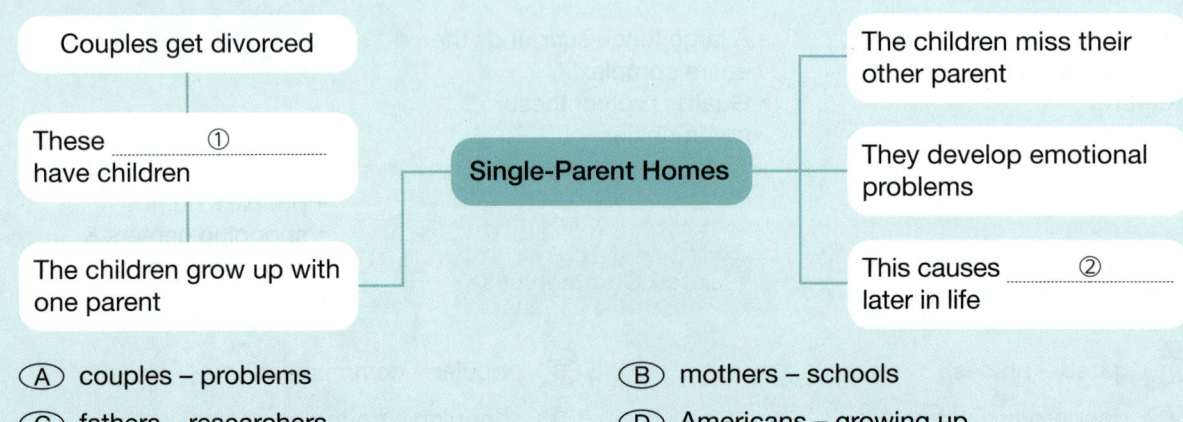

  Ⓐ couples – problems
  Ⓑ mothers – schools
  Ⓒ fathers – researchers
  Ⓓ Americans – growing up

112

• Exercise 8 •

Peer Pressure

06-09

Teenagers often experience difficult times. One of the most difficult things is peer pressure. Their peers are other teenagers. Some teenagers do activities like drinking beer or smoking. Many teenagers do not want to do these. However, bad teens have them do so. Many teens believe they will not be popular unless they do these things. So they go ahead and do these bad activities.

This can cause many problems. For example, some teenagers go to parties and drink beer. They do not really want to drink. However, sometimes they get drunk. Then, they drive their cars. So they might have accidents. Sometimes they get hurt or even die. This shows how peer pressure can be very harmful.

peer [n] an equal; a person the same age as another
pressure [n] force
drunk [adj] having had too much alcohol to drink

Q1 The word "these" in the passage refers to
Ⓐ their peers   Ⓑ other teenagers
Ⓒ activities   Ⓓ bad teens

Q2 The word "they" in the passage refers to
Ⓐ some teenagers   Ⓑ parties
Ⓒ their cars   Ⓓ accidents

Reading Skills Mapping

 What is the best answer for the blanks below?

Some teens do bad activities

One of the most difficult things for teenagers

Teenagers go to parties and get drunk

They ___①___ others to do the same things

Peer Pressure

Then, they drive their cars

They have ___②___ and get hurt or die

Ⓐ ask – parties   Ⓑ drink – cars
Ⓒ force – accidents Ⓓ smoke – problems

Grammar Point

Verbs

1 Certain verbs have infinitives as objects, and certain verbs have gerunds as objects.

○ verb + infinitive

> volunteer, try, plan, want, decide, expect, promise, hope …

- They **volunteer to work** somewhere.
- They may **try to solve** their problems.
- They also **plan to reduce** traffic.
- But they do not really **want to drink**.
- They **decided to move** to another city.

○ verb + gerund

> enjoy, begin, finish, give up, practice, avoid …

- Both children and adults **enjoy visiting** these places.
- People **began purchasing** automobiles.
- She **finished studying** for her exam.
- You should **give up drinking** and **smoking**.
- The team **practices playing** soccer after school every day.

2 Let, make, have, and get can be used to express the idea that X causes Y to do something. The causatives let, make, and have are followed by the simple form of a verb. The causative get is followed by an infinitive. The causative help is followed by an infinitive or the simple form of a verb.

- These **let** people **get** exercise and **play** team sports.
- My mother **made** me **clean** my room.
- She **had** her friend **help** her with her homework.
- I **got** my friend **to play** a game with me.
- They **help** children **learn** (**to learn**) about teamwork.

3 Some verbs have special prepositions follow them.

- The stranger **robbed** him **of** his wallet.
- She **derived** happiness **from** the story.
- We **provided** the homeless **with** shelter.
- He **informed** her **of** their abilities.
- He **prohibited** her **from** leaving.
- The boss **blamed** him **for** his lateness.

- He **deprived** her **of** that opportunity.
- He **drew** water **from** the tank.
- They **supplied** the cabinets **with** food.
- I **advised** him **of** the promise.
- John **kept** Larry **from** learning the answer.
- They **praised** her **for** her courage.

Grammar Check-Up

A Circle the parts of the sentences that are grammatically incorrect.

1. My mother <u>promised</u> <u>take</u> me <u>to</u> the <u>amusement park</u>.
               ⓐ   ⓑ   ⓒ   ⓓ
2. Please <u>do not</u> <u>blame</u> me <u>with</u> someone else's <u>mistake</u>.
          ⓐ   ⓑ   ⓒ   ⓓ
3. Mrs. Kim <u>made</u> her students <u>to</u> <u>do</u> <u>homework</u> every night.
            ⓐ   ⓑ ⓒ   ⓓ
4. We <u>started</u> <u>work</u> <u>on</u> <u>the project</u> early last morning.
          ⓐ   ⓑ ⓒ   ⓓ
5. She <u>does</u> not <u>want</u> <u>to</u> <u>going</u> to the beach this summer.
        ⓐ   ⓑ ⓒ ⓓ

B Choose the sentences that are NOT grammatically correct.

1. ⓐ The doctor supplied the patient with some medicine.
   ⓑ Everyone was prohibited from going into that room.
   ⓒ The thieves robbed the bank from its money.
   ⓓ Ken's parents praised him for his excellent performance.

2. ⓐ I want to help you improve your English ability.
   ⓑ She will let him to watch that movie.
   ⓒ Mr. Lee made them be quiet.
   ⓓ He had John put the box in the family room.

3. ⓐ You should not avoid telling your mother the news.
   ⓑ Bruce plans visiting Europe this winter.
   ⓒ I promise to tell the truth from now on.
   ⓓ They usually enjoy playing online games together.

C Choose the correct prepositions.

1. I will not blame you (of / for) this problem.
2. My mother provided me (with / to) some money for this trip.
3. He advised us (of / from) our choices.
4. Can you draw some water (from / out) the well?
5. She kept him (to / from) catching his train.

Vocabulary Review

A Circle the words that best complete the sentences.

1 (Peer / Teen) pressure can be very difficult for some teenagers.
2 It is difficult for some people to (interact / be addicted) with others.
3 People without homes often go to homeless (hospitals / shelters).
4 Miss Jacobs has a personal (vehicle / transportation) for driving to work.
5 There is a (fence / gate) going all around that house.

B Choose the best words to complete the sentences.

1 The teenagers often hang out at the shopping _____.
   - A suburb
   - B factory
   - C supermarket
   - D mall

2 Public transportation can help _____ traffic on the roads.
   - A reduce
   - B pressure
   - C show
   - D leave

3 Many church members do _____ work to help others.
   - A emotional
   - B popular
   - C charity
   - D crowded

4 The couple got a _____ and stopped living together.
   - A marriage
   - B transportation
   - C divorce
   - D researcher

5 Those students are _____ in a soccer league after school.
   - A living
   - B building
   - C performing
   - D participating

C Choose the words with the closest meanings to the highlighted words.

1 That couple often argues about many different things.
   - Ⓐ fights
   - Ⓑ experiences
   - Ⓒ misses
   - Ⓓ has

2 Steve volunteered at the hospital, so he did not get any money.
   - Ⓐ work
   - Ⓑ receive
   - Ⓒ go
   - Ⓓ run

3 The mayor is now under pressure to resign.
   - Ⓐ exercise
   - Ⓑ harm
   - Ⓒ purchase
   - Ⓓ force

4 My brothers run an Italian restaurant in Boston.
   - Ⓐ operate
   - Ⓑ got
   - Ⓒ help
   - Ⓓ surround

5 The couple had many problems between them.
   - Ⓐ decades
   - Ⓑ places
   - Ⓒ activities
   - Ⓓ issues

D Complete the sentences by filling in the blanks with the best words from the list. Change the forms of the words if necessary. Use each word only once.

| surround | decade | drawback | purchase | emotional |

1 The family lived in that house for over two _____.
2 There are many _____ to using credit cards too much.
3 The student became _____ when she won first place in the contest.
4 The fence _____ the building and keeps out unwanted people.
5 I would like to _____ a new car sometime this weekend.

Practice Test

The Changing Roles of Women

For most of history, men's and women's roles were separate. Traditionally, men were the providers. They hunted or farmed to provide food for their families. Or they worked and earned money for their families. Women, on the other hand, often remained home. They took care of their children and raised them. This was true for thousands of years. However, lately, the roles of women are changing.

First, many women are leaving their homes nowadays to work. In the past, some women worked. However, they often worked primarily as teachers, nurses, or secretaries. Then, in the nineteenth and twentieth centuries, feminism started. This theory states that men and women are equal. Thanks to feminism, many women began getting different jobs. Today, there are women doing many different jobs, including working as engineers, doctors, lawyers, and pilots.

Second, many women are not raising their children by themselves nowadays. Countless working women send their children to daycare centers. There, their children can play with other children the same age. The center takes care of their children. That way, the women can work. Fathers also sometimes stay home and take care of the children. In these cases, the woman works and earns money instead. This is very different from the traditional roles of women.

raise **v** to bring up
feminism **n** the belief that women and men are equal

1 The word "they" in the passage refers to

   Ⓐ men
   Ⓑ women
   Ⓒ their families
   Ⓓ men's and women's roles

2 According to paragraph 2, which of the following is true of women?

   Ⓐ Most of them work at home nowadays.
   Ⓑ They hunt and provide food for their families.
   Ⓒ They work many different jobs these days.
   Ⓓ They still cannot be engineers or pilots.

3 According to paragraph 2, which of the following can be inferred about feminism?

   Ⓐ It has changed many women's lives.
   Ⓑ It ended in the twentieth century.
   Ⓒ Many men disagree with it.
   Ⓓ It has helped women go to better schools.

4 The word "Countless" in the passage is closest in meaning to

   Ⓐ Numerous
   Ⓑ Several
   Ⓒ Few
   Ⓓ Some

5 The author discusses "daycare centers" in paragraph 3 in order to

   Ⓐ describe places for children better than schools
   Ⓑ discuss their costs and conditions
   Ⓒ show why men do not care for children
   Ⓓ show where working women send their children

6 *Directions:* An introductory sentence for a brief summary of the passage is provided below. Complete the summary by selecting the THREE answer choices that express the most important ideas in the passage. Some answer choices do not belong in the summary because they express ideas that are not presented in the passage or are minor ideas in the passage. *This question is worth 2 points.*

Women's roles have changed from staying home in the past to leaving the house to work in the present.

-
-
-

Answer Choices

1. Women used to stay home and care for their children.
2. Feminism was important in the twentieth century.
3. Some fathers now stay home to raise their children.
4. Women have many different jobs nowadays.
5. Daycare centers help take care of children in the day.
6. Some women get jobs as doctors and lawyers these days.

CHAPTER 07

Exploration
(Identifying Cohesive Devices)

1. Christopher Columbus
2. John Cabot
3. Ponce de Leon
4. James Cook
5. The Vikings
6. Marco Polo
7. Undersea Exploration
8. Maps

CHAPTER 7 **Exploration** (Identifying Cohesive Devices)

Understanding TOEFL Question Types & Reading Skills

1 Question Types — Sentence Simplification & Insert Text Questions

- *Sentence Simplification questions* ask you to look at a sentence from the passage. Then you must choose a shorter version of the sentence that has the same meaning. You need to recognize which words are important and which ones you can omit from the sentence.
- *Insert Text questions* ask you to look at a sentence not in the passage. You must then decide where in the passage you could include the new sentence. For this question, you should be able to understand how ideas logically connect to each other.

- **Example Sentence Simplification & Insert Text Questions**
  - Which of the following best expresses the essential information in the highlighted sentence? *Incorrect* answer choices change the meaning in important ways or leave out essential information.
  - Look at the four squares [■] that indicate where the following sentence could be added to the passage.

    [You will see a sentence in bold.]

    Where would the sentence best fit?
    Click on a square [■] to add the sentence to the passage.

- **Useful Tips for Your Success**

▶ Learn to	→	identify synonyms of various words.
	→	recognize important connector words.
▶ Don't	→	choose answers that only provide half of a sentence's meaning.
	→	insert sentences where they make no sense logically.

Sample Question

Space Exploration

People have long desired to explore outer space. In 1957, the first satellite went into orbit. In addition, men have gone into space. And others have explored the moon. <mark>In the future, men will surely explore Mars and the other planets.</mark>

desire [v] to want; to wish
orbit [n] a course; a path

Q Which of the following best expresses the essential information in the highlighted sentence? *Incorrect* answer choices change the meaning in important ways or leave out essential information.

- Ⓐ People will visit other planets in the future.
- Ⓑ Men have already visited Mars and other planets.
- Ⓒ The exploration of Mars is happening now.
- Ⓓ People now are living on Mars and some other planets.

2 Reading Skills — Identifying Cohesive Devices

Identifying cohesive devices is an important skill that will show you how writers connect different ideas. These cohesive devices allow readers to understand how one idea leads to another. When writers use these ideas, they make their passages more logical and easier to understand.

Check-Up

▶ Choose the best conjunction in the box below to complete the sentences.

| but | for example | in addition | because |

In 1957, the first satellite went into orbit. _____, men have gone into space. And others have explored the moon.

Chapter ❼ 123

• **Exercise 1** •

Christopher Columbus

🎧 07-02

Christopher Columbus was an explorer from Italy. In 1492, he sailed across the vast Atlantic Ocean. He had three ships with him. They were the *Pinta*, the *Nina*, and the *Santa Maria*. After over eight weeks, he made it to America. Later, Columbus made three more voyages to the New World. Thanks to Columbus, many other men also sailed to the Americas.

vast adj wide; immense
voyage n a trip; a journey

Q Which of the following best expresses the essential information in the highlighted sentence? *Incorrect* answer choices change the meaning in important ways or leave out essential information.

Ⓐ He spent eight weeks in America.
Ⓑ It took two months to reach America.
Ⓒ He went to America in under eight weeks.
Ⓓ He lived in America for two months.

Reading Skills Identifying Cohesive Devices

 **Check-Up** In the passage, the pronoun "They" in the sentence, "They were the *Pinta*, the *Nina*, and the *Santa Maria*," refers to _____.

Ⓐ other men
Ⓑ ships
Ⓒ voyages
Ⓓ the Americas

Exercise 2

John Cabot

In 1497, John Cabot departed England. He sailed west across the Atlantic Ocean. He was hoping to reach Asia. Instead, he discovered Canada. And he was the first European there since the Vikings many centuries before. **1** The next year, Cabot sailed back across the Atlantic. **2** One of his five ships stopped in Ireland. **3** But the other four disappeared. **4** Nobody knows what happened to Cabot and his men.

depart v to leave
century n a period of 100 years

Q Look at the four squares [■] that indicate where the following sentence could be added to the passage.

His trip was considered a great success.

Where would the sentence best fit?

Reading Skills — Identifying Cohesive Devices

Check-Up Choose the best conjunctions in the box below to complete the sentences.

but   and   or   because

1 Instead, he discovered Canada. _____ he was the first European there since the Vikings many centuries before.

2 One of his five ships stopped in Ireland. _____ the other four disappeared.

• **Exercise 3** •

Ponce de Leon

Ponce de Leon was a sixteenth-century Spanish explorer. He was different from most New World explorers. He wanted neither gold nor fame. Instead, he sought the Fountain of Youth. People also called it the "Water of Life." He believed it made people young. During his travels, he discovered Florida. He thought the fountain was there. However, he never found it.

fame n popularity; celebrity
seek v to search for; to hunt

Q Which of the following best expresses the essential information in the highlighted sentence? *Incorrect* answer choices change the meaning in important ways or leave out essential information.

A All New World explorers were different.
B He was the same as everyone else.
C He was not like other New World voyagers.
D The New World made him very different.

Reading Skills Identifying Cohesive Devices

Check-Up In the passage, the pronoun "it" in the sentence, "He believed it made people young," refers to _____.

A New World
B gold
C fame
D the Fountain of Youth

• **Exercise 4** •

James Cook

James Cook was an important British explorer. He spent more than ten years sailing the Pacific Ocean. And he charted the coast of Australia. This helped map the continent. **1** He also discovered many island groups in the region. **2** Furthermore, he was the first European to land in Hawaii. **3** He named the islands the Sandwich Islands. **4**

chart v to map
furthermore adv additionally; moreover

Q Look at the four squares [■] that indicate where the following sentence could be added to the passage.

Unfortunately, he died fighting some islanders on a trip there.

Where would the sentence best fit?

Reading Skills | **Identifying Cohesive Devices**

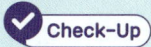 Choose the best conjunctions in the box below to complete the sentences.

| but   and   furthermore   because |

1 He spent more than ten years sailing the Pacific Ocean. _____ he charted the coast of Australia.
2 He also discovered many island groups in the region. _____, he was the first European to land in Hawaii

• **Exercise 5** •

The Vikings

The Vikings were from northern Europe. They were fierce warriors and fighters. And they loved sailing the oceans. They were also great explorers. From the eighth to eleventh centuries, they sailed all around the Atlantic Ocean. They visited England. They even went to Constantinople and Russia.

They also sailed across the Atlantic Ocean. In 986, they landed on Greenland. Erik the Red and his son Leif Eriksson made it there. ■1 However, they continued sailing west. ■2 They eventually visited North America. ■3 They were the first Europeans to visit North America. ■4 But the Vikings did not remain there. Instead, they returned to Europe. So no one knew about America for a very long time.

fierce adj ferocious; violent
warrior n a fighter; a soldier
remain v to stay

Q1 Which of the following best expresses the essential information in the highlighted sentence? *Incorrect* answer choices change the meaning in important ways or leave out essential information.

Ⓐ They sailed the Atlantic Ocean for hundreds of years.
Ⓑ For several centuries, they discovered the Atlantic Ocean.
Ⓒ Only the Vikings sailed the Atlantic Ocean for four centuries.
Ⓓ In the eighth and eleventh centuries, they sailed the Atlantic Ocean.

Q2 Look at the four squares [■] that indicate where the following sentence could be added to the passage.

These two men brought a small group of Vikings with them.

Where would the sentence best fit?

Reading Skills Identifying Cohesive Devices

 **Check-Up**) In paragraph 2, the pronoun "they" in the sentence, "Instead, they returned to Europe," refers to _____.

Ⓐ Constantinople and Russia
Ⓑ Erik the Red and his son Leif Eriksson
Ⓒ Europeans
Ⓓ the Vikings

128

Exercise 6

Marco Polo

In the thirteenth century, most Europeans knew nothing about Asia. But they were extremely curious about it. Therefore, a few of them traveled east. But many of them did not return. Marco Polo was an Italian adventurer. He traveled east to Asia on the Silk Road. No one saw him for years. So people believed he was dead. But, suddenly, after twenty-four years, Marco Polo returned to Europe.

He had traveled all the way to China. ■1 He met the Mongol Kublai Khan. ■2 He actually became the khan's advisor. ■3 He became very wealthy in Asia. ■4 But he still wanted to go home. After he returned, many people heard about his trip. So more and more Europeans began visiting Asia.

curious adj inquisitive
adventurer n a traveler; an explorer
wealthy adj rich

Q1 Which of the following best expresses the essential information in the highlighted sentence? *Incorrect* answer choices change the meaning in important ways or leave out essential information.

Ⓐ Marco Polo went to Europe at the age of twenty-four.
Ⓑ Marco Polo lived in Europe for over twenty years.
Ⓒ Marco Polo made more than twenty trips to Europe.
Ⓓ Marco Polo went back to Europe after many years.

Q2 Look at the four squares [■] that indicate where the following sentence could be added to the passage.

On his way there, he had many adventures.

Where would the sentence best fit?

Reading Skills Identifying Cohesive Devices

Check-Up Choose the best conjunctions in the box below to complete the sentences.

> after   but   and   so

1 No one saw him for years. _____ people believed he was dead.
2 But he still wanted to go home. _____ he returned, many people heard about his trip.

• **Exercise 7** •

Undersea Exploration

🎧 07-08

Men have explored most of the Earth's surface. ■1 However, there is still one place most men have not visited. ■2 This is the area under the ocean. ■3 The ocean still remains a mysterious place. ■4 But now more people are learning its secrets. They do this in several ways.

Some people use scuba diving equipment. They wear it while swimming. This allows them to breathe underwater. Other people explore the oceans in submarines. Submarines can travel underwater. Some can stay under the ocean for months. Thanks to submarines, people have learned very much about the ocean. There are also other submersible vehicles. These can dive deep under the ocean. They have discovered many new species of fish.

mysterious [adj] strange; unknown
thanks to [phr] because of; on account of

Q1 Look at the four squares [■] that indicate where the following sentence could be added to the passage.

In fact, they know very much about it now.

Where would the sentence best fit?

Q2 Which of the following best expresses the essential information in the highlighted sentence? *Incorrect* answer choices change the meaning in important ways or leave out essential information.

Ⓐ People did not know about the ocean until submarines.
Ⓑ In submarines, everyone can learn about the ocean.
Ⓒ Submarines have helped people learn about the ocean.
Ⓓ There are many submarines in the ocean.

Reading Skills Identifying Cohesive Devices

 In paragraph 1, the pronoun "its" in the sentence, "But now more people are learning its secrets," refers to _____ .

Ⓐ the Earth's surface
Ⓑ one place
Ⓒ the ocean
Ⓓ scuba diving equipment

Exercise 8

Maps

Without maps, people can become lost easily. So maps are crucial for explorers. **1** Their maps have to be very accurate. **2** Unfortunately, a long time ago, many maps had incorrect information. **3** Or they showed wrong distances between things. **4**

The most common kinds of maps are geographical maps. These show one particular area of land. This region may be very large or small. The smaller the area, the more detail the map has. The scale of the map is very important. This shows how close objects are to one another.

Thanks to maps, man's knowledge of the Earth increased greatly. As people began exploring more, their maps became better. Nowadays, the maps people use are typically high in quality.

accurate adj exact; precise   **geographical** adj relating to geography; physical

Q1 Look at the four squares [] that indicate where the following sentence could be added to the passage.

These problems often caused people to become very confused.

Where would the sentence best fit?

Q2 Which of the following best expresses the essential information in the highlighted sentence? *Incorrect* answer choices change the meaning in important ways or leave out essential information.

Ⓐ Many explorers made better maps.
Ⓑ Maps improved with more explorations.
Ⓒ There are more explorers with better maps.
Ⓓ Maps are always getting better for explorers.

Reading Skills Identifying Cohesive Devices

Check-Up Choose the best conjunctions in the box below to complete the sentences.

> before   as   because   or

1 Unfortunately, a long time ago, many maps had incorrect information. _____ they showed wrong distances between things.

2 Thanks to maps, man's knowledge of the Earth increased greatly. _____ people began exploring more, their maps became better.

Prepositions

Grammar Point

1. **Prepositions of time** relate a specific point or period of time.

2. **Prepositions of place** show the location of something or someone.

	Prepositions	Example Sentences
Prepositions of Time	at + times, festivals, mealtimes, and specific periods	• We always eat lunch at twelve o'clock.
	in + seasons, years, months, and parts of the day	• My mother's birthday is in August.
	on + days, dates, and special days	• Christmas is on December 25.
	until + when a situation ends	• The class lasted until three o'clock.
	by + when something happens before a time	• You need to send me that file by this evening.
	before + earlier than something	• She saw him before the lecture.
	after + later than something	• He left the movie after one hour.
Prepositions of Place	at + places as a point in space	• They arrived at the airport.
	in / on / over / under / in front of / behind / next to / between	• The ball is in the box. • The ball is on the box. • A cat jumps over the fence. • A cat is under the tree. • A girl is in front of the car. • A boy is behind the car. • There is a bench next to a tree. • There is a bench between the tree and the house.
Other Prepositions	with + a tool or an object	• Jane hit the nail with a hammer.
	by + most forms of transportation	• We are going there by car.
	of + the materials that form something	• This ring is made of gold.
	from + a substance that has been used to make something	• We get beefsteak from cows.
	to + direction	• My family went to the park.
	for + direction	• They started for the restaurant.

132

Grammar Check-Up

A Choose the correct prepositions that best complete the sentences.

1 You need to finish your homework (at / by) tomorrow morning.
2 Her birthday is (on / in) September 26.
3 Jason keeps his clothes (in / under) his closet.
4 How can we get (to / at) the downtown area?
5 Do not call me (from / until) the game is over.

B Complete the sentences by using the words in the box.

> over   by   after   on   front

1 What are you going to do _____ your birthday?
2 Can you jump _____ this box?
3 They met each other _____ dinner.
4 They are going to go to that city _____ train.
5 Please do not stand right in _____ of the television.

C Read the following story and fill in the blanks with the prepositions in the box. Use each word only once.

> until   before   for   by   on   in   on

Lisa's family wanted to take a trip. So they decided to go to the beach _____ car. They went on their vacation _____ summer. They planned to stay there _____ the end of summer vacation. So they left their house _____ August 5. Lisa's father wanted to leave _____ breakfast. But Lisa's brother felt bad. So they left after lunch instead. They started driving _____ the beach. They drove all day long _____ that day. Everyone was happy when they finally made it to the beach.

Vocabulary Review

A Circle the words that best complete the sentences.

1 There are many different (submersible / **species**) of animals on the Earth.
2 He became (**extremely** / accurately) rich when he won the lottery.
3 The Atlantic Ocean is a very (**vast** / fierce) body of water.
4 Scuba diving (**equipment** / explorer) lets people breathe underwater.
5 The explorers (visited / **traveled**) across Asia and got to China.

B Choose the best words to complete the sentences.

1 Many people are interested in exploring outer _____.
   A space
   B moon
   C planet
   D Mars

2 Martin _____ thought of the answer to the question.
   A extremely
   B quality
   C greatly
   D suddenly

3 The boat _____ on the sea for over three months.
   A explored
   B visited
   C showed
   D sailed

4 People are often _____ about things they know nothing about.
   A wealthy
   B curious
   C mysterious
   D fierce

5 No one wanted to _____ in the strange land all alone.
   A return
   B breathe
   C remain
   D discover

C Choose the words with the closest meanings to the highlighted words.

1. They are hoping to find silver in the mountains.
   - Ⓐ return
   - Ⓑ discover
   - Ⓒ explore
   - Ⓓ show

2. A lot of explorers desired to become wealthy.
   - Ⓐ loved
   - Ⓑ sailed
   - Ⓒ continued
   - Ⓓ wanted

3. There were many warriors in the army.
   - Ⓐ explorers
   - Ⓑ submarines
   - Ⓒ fighters
   - Ⓓ Vikings

4. During his travels, he saw many interesting places.
   - Ⓐ voyages
   - Ⓑ species
   - Ⓒ advisors
   - Ⓓ groups

5. The captain charted all of the places he had visited.
   - Ⓐ mapped
   - Ⓑ began
   - Ⓒ sought
   - Ⓓ found

D Complete the sentences by filling in the blanks with the best words from the list. Change the forms of the words if necessary. Use each word only once.

| planet | secret | submersible | mysterious | discover |

1. A submarine is a kind of _____ vehicle.
2. Emily was very good at keeping _____ from other people.
3. The people will _____ plants and animals on their trip to the jungle.
4. Many satellites have gone to explore other _____ in the solar system.
5. Someone found a _____ message hidden in the treasure chest.

Practice Test

The Lewis and Clark Expedition

At the end of the eighteenth century, the United States was still a small country. It was mostly just land east of the Mississippi River. However, this changed in 1803. That year, President Thomas Jefferson made the Louisiana Purchase from Napoleon in France. **1** This was an enormous piece of land. **2** It covered the area in the middle of the present-day United States. **3** Jefferson wanted to explore the new territory. **4** So he sent out the Lewis and Clark expedition.

Meriwether Lewis and William Clark were its two leaders. They set out in 1804. They would not return until 1806. Their group had several goals. They were to explore the Louisiana Territory and to learn about its plants and animals. They were to study its Indian tribes. They were also to try to find a passage to the Pacific Ocean. They accomplished all their goals.

However, the trip was not easy. They encountered many difficulties along the way. They traveled by boat sometimes. But they often had to walk overland. They met many Indian tribes. Fortunately, most of them were friendly. The two winters they spent in the wilderness were very difficult. Still, they managed to reach the Pacific Ocean and then return to the east. This opened the door for further exploration by many others.

encounter v to meet; to run into
wilderness n an area without many people

1. The word "its" in the passage refers to
   - Ⓐ the new territory
   - Ⓑ the Lewis and Clark expedition
   - Ⓒ Meriwether Lewis
   - Ⓓ William Clark

2. The word "goals" in the passage is closest in meaning to
   - Ⓐ patterns
   - Ⓑ methods
   - Ⓒ objectives
   - Ⓓ ways

3. The author discusses "many difficulties" in paragraph 3 in order to
   - Ⓐ explain why the Indians were unfriendly
   - Ⓑ prove the trip west was not very easy
   - Ⓒ show why people began moving west
   - Ⓓ note why the trip took a long time

4. According to paragraph 3, which of the following is true of the Lewis and Clark expedition?
   - Ⓐ They always traveled by boat.
   - Ⓑ They met only a few Indians.
   - Ⓒ They sailed on the Pacific Ocean.
   - Ⓓ They spent two winters on their trip.

5. Look at the four squares [■] that indicate where the following sentence could be added to the passage.

   Only a few people had ever been to this unknown land before.

   Where would the sentence best fit?
   Click on a square [■] to add the sentence to the passage.

6 *Directions:* An introductory sentence for a brief summary of the passage is provided below. Complete the summary by selecting the THREE answer choices that express the most important ideas in the passage. Some answer choices do not belong in the summary because they express ideas that are not presented in the passage or are minor ideas in the passage. *This question is worth 2 points.*

The Lewis and Clark expedition encountered many difficulties but taught people very much about the Louisiana Territory.

-
-
-

Answer Choices

1. President Jefferson ordered Lewis and Clark to lead the expedition.
2. The expedition learned about the plants and animals there.
3. The men often had to walk on land to go west.
4. The United States bought the land from France.
5. They sometimes got into fights with the Indians.
6. The expedition discovered a way to the Pacific Ocean.

CHAPTER 08

Environment
(Outlining)

1. Rainforests
2. Recycling
3. Acid Rain
4. Erosion
5. Reducing Garbage
6. Hurricanes and Typhoons
7. Stopping Deforestation
8. Global Warming

CHAPTER 8 Environment (Outlining)

Understanding TOEFL Question Types & Reading Skills

1 Question Types — Prose Summary & Fill in a Table Questions

- *Prose Summary questions* test your ability to detect the major ideas in the passage. You must be able to find the major ideas and ignore the minor ideas.
- *Fill in a Table questions* ask you to complete a table that classifies various parts of the passage. You must be able to find the major ideas in the passage and then classify them according to the topic.

● Example Prose Summary & Fill in a Table Questions

- An introductory sentence for a brief summary of the passage is provided below. Complete the summary by selecting the THREE answer choices that express the most important ideas in the passage.
- Complete the table below to summarize information about X discussed in the passage. Match the appropriate statements to X with which they are associated.

● Useful Tips for Your Success

- Learn to → find the main ideas in the passage.
  → recognize the facts associated with the main ideas.
- Don't → pay attention to the minor ideas.
  → become confused between major and minor ideas.

Sample Question

Fuels

🎧 08-01

Fuels are important energy sources. One kind is liquid fuel. This comes from dead plants and animals. The most common liquid fuel is gasoline. Another type is diesel fuel. Vehicles utilize these types of fuels. Additionally, there are solid fuels. People use these fuels to create energy and to heat buildings. Wood and coal are two of these types of fuels.

fuel n something that creates energy   **utilize** v to use

Q1 An introductory sentence for a brief summary of the passage is provided below. Complete the summary by selecting the TWO answer choices that express the most important ideas in the passage.

Fuels are important forms of energy on the Earth.

- Ⓐ There are no more fossil fuels left on the Earth.
- Ⓑ Gasoline and diesel are liquid fuels.
- Ⓒ Common solid fuels are wood and coal.
- Ⓓ Vehicles use fuel.

Q2 Complete the table below by matching.

Liquid Fuels	Solid Fuels

Ⓐ gasoline   Ⓑ coal   Ⓒ wood   Ⓓ diesel

2 Reading Skills — Outlining

Outlining can identify both the major and minor ideas in a passage. Use outlines to organize all of the ideas in the passage. Then, you can show the relationships between all of these ideas.

Check-Up

▶ **Complete the following outline.**

I Liquid fuel: comes from dead animals and _____
   • Gasoline and diesel are liquid fuels.

II Solid fuel: also creates energy and heats buildings
   • Common solid fuels are _____ and wood.

• **Exercise 1** •

Rainforests

🎧 08-02

    Rainforests are some of the most unique places on the Earth. They are highly diverse places. Many species of animals live there. Mammals, birds, and reptiles all live in these forests.

    Rainforests like the Amazon have countless species of trees and plants. They help create a majority of the Earth's oxygen supply. Without rainforests, the Earth would be a very different place.

---

diverse adj varied; different
countless adj numerous
reptile n a cold-blooded animal like a snake or lizard

Q An introductory sentence for a brief summary of the passage is provided below. Complete the summary by selecting the TWO answer choices that express the most important ideas in the passage.

Rainforests are unique and important places.

Ⓐ Rainforests provide much of the Earth's oxygen.
Ⓑ There is a rainforest in the Amazon.
Ⓒ Many kinds of animals live in rainforests.
Ⓓ People visit rainforests to see different animal species.

Reading Skills Outlining

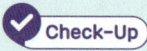 **Complete the following outline.**

I Many species of animals
  1. Mammals
  2. Birds
  3. _____

II Many trees and plants
  1. Create much of the Earth's _____

142

• **Exercise 2** •

Recycling

08-03

People use too many natural resources. The Earth's supply is running out. So recycling is very important. By doing that, companies can reuse the Earth's resources over and over.

People can recycle many things. They can recycle glass from bottles and paper from newspapers and magazines. They can also recycle metal from cans. By recycling, people can help save the Earth's resources.

run out phr to exhaust; to use up
reuse v to use again

Q An introductory sentence for a brief summary of the passage is provided below. Complete the summary by selecting the TWO answer choices that express the most important ideas in the passage.

People can recycle many different objects.
- Ⓐ Some people recycle metal and paper.
- Ⓑ Many individuals never recycle.
- Ⓒ Most people do not save natural resources.
- Ⓓ Recycling helps preserve natural resources.

Reading Skills | Outlining

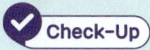 **Check-Up** Complete the following outline.

I The Earth's natural resources are running out.

II People can recycle many things.
   1. Glass from _____
   2. Paper from newspapers and magazines
   3. Metal from _____

III People can help save the Earth's resources by _____

• **Exercise 3** •

Acid Rain

🎧 08-04

Sometimes pollution rises into the atmosphere. Clouds typically absorb it. Later, rain falls from these clouds. But this rain is dirty and harmful. People call it acid rain.

Acid rain kills many animals. Thanks to acid rain, some lakes have no life. Nowadays, people are trying to prevent acid rain. But it is still a problem in various places.

atmosphere　**n**　the air
prevent　**v**　to stop; to keep from happening

Q An introductory sentence for a brief summary of the passage is provided below. Complete the summary by selecting the TWO answer choices that express the most important ideas in the passage.

Acid rain is very harmful to the environment.

Ⓐ People cannot really stop it.
Ⓑ It can kill many creatures.
Ⓒ People are trying to prevent acid rain.
Ⓓ It often kills all life in lakes.

Reading Skills　Outlining

 **Complete the following outline.**

I Pollution rises into the atmosphere.
　1. _____ typically absorb this pollution.
　2. Later, rain falls from these _____

II Acid rain is harmful.
　1. Kills animals
　2. No life in some _____

III People try to prevent this rain.

144

• **Exercise 4** •

Erosion

Erosion happens when the land gets worn away. Water, wind, and ice can often do this. They can change how the land looks. Erosion can happen slowly. For example, it may take place over thousands of years. Or it can happen quickly. A hurricane can erode land in hours. Due to erosion, the face of the land is constantly changing.

wear away phr to break down
face n the outer part of something

Q An introductory sentence for a brief summary of the passage is provided below. Complete the summary by selecting the TWO answer choices that express the most important ideas in the passage.

Erosion changes how the land appears.

Ⓐ Hurricanes make a lot of rain fall.
Ⓑ Erosion can wear down the land.
Ⓒ Water, wind, and ice can cause erosion.
Ⓓ Sometimes erosion happens slowly.

Reading Skills Outlining

Check-Up Complete the following outline.

I Erosion happens when the land gets worn away.
II How erosion happens
  1. Wind, _____, and ice
  2. Can happen slowly or quickly
  3. Makes the _____ of the land change constantly

• **Exercise 5** •

Reducing Garbage

 08-06

Garbage is an enormous problem nowadays. So people need to think of ways to stop making so much garbage. They can reduce garbage in two places. They can do this in their homes and outside their homes.

First, people should stop making so much trash at home. They can try to recycle glass, paper, plastic, and metal. They can reuse cloth napkins instead of paper napkins. People can also purchase rechargeable batteries. Then people will not have to throw them away.

Outside their homes, they can do many things. They can bring their own bags to grocery stores instead of receiving new ones. People can also buy used items.

enormous **adj** huge
recycle **v** to reuse

Q Complete the table below to summarize information about reducing garbage discussed in the passage. Match the appropriate statements to the places to reduce garbage.

At Home	Outside the Home
•	•
•	•

Statements

Ⓐ People can use cloth napkins.
Ⓑ Everyone can eat less food.
Ⓒ Everyone can bring bags to grocery stores.
Ⓓ People can buy used products.
Ⓔ People can use paper napkins.
Ⓕ Everyone can try to recycle.

Reading Skills Outlining

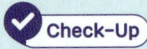 **Complete the following outline.**

I People can reduce garbage.

II In people's homes
   1. Try to recycle glass, paper, plastic, and metal
   2. Use _____ instead of paper napkins
   3. Purchase rechargeable _____

III Outside people's homes
   1. Bring _____ to grocery stores
   2. Purchase _____

• **Exercise 6** •

Hurricanes and Typhoons

08-07

Nature can be very violent. Great storms often suddenly form. Two kinds of storms are hurricanes and typhoons. They are really the same kind of storm. However, hurricanes form in the Atlantic Ocean and the eastern Pacific Ocean. And typhoons form in the western Pacific Ocean.

Hurricanes affect countries like the United States, Cuba, Spain, and Brazil. They often cause great damage. In 2005, Hurricane Katrina landed in the U.S. It damaged the city of New Orleans very much. It killed around 2,000 people.

In Asia, typhoons affect countries like China, Korea, Japan, and the Philippines. They typically cause bad flooding. They can also kill many people. In 2003, Super Typhoon Maemi hit South Korea. 115 people died during it.

violent adj fierce; strong   **flooding** n a time when water covers land it usually does not

Q Complete the table below to summarize information about hurricanes and typhoons discussed in the passage. Match the appropriate statements to the type of storm they refer to.

Hurricanes	Typhoons
•	•
•	•

Statements

Ⓐ These storms form in cold water.
Ⓑ They often cause bad flooding.
Ⓒ These storms affect Cuba and Brazil.
Ⓓ They form in the western Pacific Ocean.
Ⓔ They happen in the Atlantic Ocean.
Ⓕ These storms do not usually kill people.

Reading Skills | **Outlining**

 **Check-Up** Complete the following outline.

I Two kinds of storms are hurricanes and typhoons.

II Hurricanes
　1. Form in the _____ and the eastern Pacific Ocean
　2. Affect countries like the United States, Cuba, Spain, and Brazil
　3. Hurricane _____ killed around 2,000 people in the U.S. in 2005.

III Typhoons
　1. Form in the western _____
　2. Affect countries like China, Korea, Japan, and the Philippines
　3. Typhoon _____ killed 115 people in South Korea in 2003.

Chapter 8   147

Exercise 7

Stopping Deforestation

08-08

Many places on the Earth have large forested areas. But these forests are rapidly disappearing. The reason for this is deforestation. People are simply cutting down too many trees. Deforestation is a big problem. But there are some ways to stop it.

First, some countries ban logging in certain areas. This means that loggers cannot cut down trees. This gives forests time to grow back.

Many logging companies also plant new trees. Trees are renewable resources. So people can use them again and again. By planting trees, logging companies will be able to cut down more in the future.

Deforestation is a gigantic problem. But people are slowly finding ways to stop it from happening.

---

forested adj having many trees or forests
ban v to make illegal
renewable adj able to be used again

Q Complete the table below to summarize information about deforestation discussed in the passage. Match the appropriate statements to the problems or solutions of deforestation.

Problems	Solutions
•	•
•	•

Statements

Ⓐ It is a very big problem.
Ⓑ Some countries do not allow logging.
Ⓒ Forests are rapidly disappearing.
Ⓓ The Earth has many forests.
Ⓔ People often cut down too many trees.
Ⓕ Some logging companies are planting more trees.

Reading Skills Outlining

 Complete the following outline.

I Forests are rapidly disappearing.
   1. People cut down forests.

II There are some ways to stop deforestation.
   1. Some countries ban _____ in certain areas.
   2. Many logging companies _____ new trees.

• **Exercise 8** •

Global Warming

The Earth's temperature is always changing. Sometimes it is very cold. People call these times ice ages. But sometimes it becomes hotter. People refer to these times as global warming. Lately, the Earth's temperature is warming. Some people believe humans are causing this. Others believe this is a natural occurrence.

Many people think humans produce too much carbon dioxide. Carbon dioxide goes into the air. It traps the sun's heat. So the heat cannot leave the Earth. For some people, this is the reason for global warming. Others believe the sun is getting hotter. They say other planets' temperatures are rising, too. So global warming cannot be manmade. No one knows the real reason for sure. But scientists will continue studying global warming.

refer to phr to call; to name
trap v to capture something
occurrence n an event

Q Complete the table below to summarize information about global warming discussed in the passage. Match the appropriate statements to the reason for global warming.

Manmade Global Warming	Natural Global Warming
•	•
•	•

Statements

Ⓐ The temperature is changing on the Earth.
Ⓑ Other planets' temperatures are rising.
Ⓒ There is too much carbon dioxide on the Earth.
Ⓓ Scientists will continue to study global warming.
Ⓔ The sun is getting hotter.
Ⓕ Carbon dioxide is trapping heat on the Earth.

Reading Skills | **Outlining**

 Complete the following outline.

I The Earth's temperature is always changing.
 • Sometimes it is hot, and sometimes it is cold.

II Manmade global warming
 • People create too much _____ dioxide.

III Natural global warming
 • The _____ is getting hotter.

Grammar Point

Making Sentences

	The Principles of Making Sentences	
Coherence	• Sally always goes to <u>their</u> school in the morning. • Mr. Taylor likes to go out with <u>her</u> wife.	X
	• Sally always goes to *her* school in the morning. • Mr. Taylor likes to go out with *his* wife.	O
	• I <u>am</u> at work, but David <u>was</u> still at home. • Kevin <u>is</u> working, and they <u>were</u> studying.	X
	• I *am* at work, but David *is* still at home. • Kevin *is* working, and they *are* studying.	O
	• They were <u>interested</u> learning about American history. • We <u>talked</u> many things last night.	X
	• They were *interested in* learning about American history. • We *talked about* many things last night.	O
Shortness	• The employees <u>cooperated together</u> on the project. • The teacher <u>entered into</u> the classroom.	X
	• The employees *cooperated* on the project. • The teacher *entered* the classroom.	O
	• <u>Although</u> he plays soccer every day, <u>but</u> he is not very good. • <u>And</u> they met John, <u>and</u> then they went to the game.	X
	• *Although* he plays soccer every day, he is not very good. • They met John, *and* then they went to the game.	O
	• I <u>returned back</u> to my house. • The hikers <u>climbed up</u> the mountain.	X
	• I *returned* to my house. • The hikers *climbed* the mountain.	O
	• <u>My friend he</u> always calls me on the phone. • <u>Those guys they</u> are really fun to hang out with.	X
	• *My friend* always calls me on the phone. • *Those guys* are really fun to hang out with.	O
Logicality	• My mother told me <u>frequently</u> to be quiet.	X
	• My mother *frequently* told me to be quiet. • My mother told me to be quiet *frequently*.	O

✓ Grammar Check-Up

A Circle the parts of the sentences that are grammatically incorrect.

1 We <u>opened</u> the door <u>and</u> entered <u>into</u> <u>the</u> building.
      ⓐ   ⓑ   ⓒ ⓓ

2 <u>My brother</u> and I <u>we</u> always <u>go swimming</u> <u>in</u> the lake.
    ⓐ   ⓑ   ⓒ   ⓓ

3 Harry <u>loves</u> chocolate <u>ice cream</u>, <u>but</u> Mary likes it, <u>too</u>.
       ⓐ   ⓑ   ⓒ   ⓓ

4 The students were <u>boring</u> in <u>their</u> class <u>because</u> the teacher was not <u>fun</u>.
                    ⓐ   ⓑ   ⓒ   ⓓ

5 <u>Always</u> Mr. Simmons <u>goes</u> <u>to work</u> at eight <u>in</u> the morning.
    ⓐ   ⓑ   ⓒ   ⓓ

B Choose the sentences that are NOT grammatically correct.

1 ⓐ Please be quietly.
   ⓑ Let's go home now.
   ⓒ Don't say that.
   ⓓ Be careful.

2 ⓐ He went to Busan all by themselves.
   ⓑ Susan wants to talk to her friend.
   ⓒ We ate lunch together with our teacher.
   ⓓ Larry doesn't like his math class very much.

3 ⓐ Miss Lee doesn't take trips very often.
   ⓑ I always eat three times a day.
   ⓒ She speaks rarely to other people.
   ⓓ Sometimes the students play soccer in gym class.

4 ⓐ After we watched the game, we went to see a movie.
   ⓑ I don't like spaghetti, so we didn't go to the Italian restaurant.
   ⓒ You need to work harder, or you will get a bad grade.
   ⓓ Her brother lives in Europe, so he does not enjoy it there.

5 ⓐ School is often interesting for most students.
   ⓑ Going to an amusement park is always fun.
   ⓒ Everyone thought that the story was very excited.
   ⓓ She was bored, so she turned on the television.

Vocabulary Review

A Circle the words that best complete the sentences.

1 The company (prevents / **produces**) many very valuable objects.
2 Water is a (global / **renewable**) resource people can use many times.
3 (Atmosphere / **Deforestation**) is chopping down too many trees.
4 Jason (**typically** / highly) wakes up at seven in the morning.
5 Wool (bans / **traps**) your body heat, making you warm.

B Choose the best words to complete the sentences.

1 People often recycle bottles to get more _____.

   A paper
   B glass
   C metal
   D magazines

2 Water _____ kills many creatures living in lakes and rivers.

   A atmosphere
   B temperature
   C dioxide
   D pollution

3 Please put your _____ in the garbage can.

   A logger
   B trash
   C fuel
   D resources

4 Everyone should _____ to help save natural resources.

   A recycle
   B use
   C create
   D believe

5 The government _____ people from fishing in the lake.

   A trapped
   B produced
   C affected
   D banned

C Choose the words with the closest meanings to the highlighted words.

1. The hurricane caused very much damage to the city.
   - A ocean
   - B flood
   - C sea
   - D storm

2. Janet has many diverse hobbies and interests.
   - A enormous
   - B forested
   - C different
   - D gigantic

3. This lake is manmade because of the dam on the river.
   - A artificial
   - B enormous
   - C beautiful
   - D unique

4. The atmosphere is so dirty that it is hard to breathe.
   - A sun
   - B air
   - C typhoon
   - D water

5. Mary wants to purchase a new car this weekend.
   - A rise
   - B buy
   - C change
   - D supply

D Complete the sentences by filling in the blanks with the best words from the list. Change the forms of the words if necessary. Use each word only once.

| countless | planet | typhoon | constantly | cloud |

1. The _____ lasted for four days and dropped a lot of rain.
2. It was a perfect day as there were no _____ in the sky.
3. There are eight _____ in the solar system.
4. The forest _____ changes as trees and other plants grow and die.
5. _____ numbers of animals live in the forest.

Practice Test

Renewable Energy Sources

During the twentieth century, people began using many new machines. These machines, like cars and airplanes, use great amounts of energy. For the most part, people created the energy needed from oil or natural gas. However, many scientists today believe the world's supply of oil and gas is running out. So people are looking for other sources of energy. Some promising ones are renewable energies.

Renewable energy is energy people can use again. There are many kinds of renewable energy sources. Water is one of them. There are numerous dams using water to create hydroelectric energy. The water in the rivers is continually flowing. So people can use it again and again to create electricity.

The sun is another source of renewable energy. Solar energy is energy people create by using the sun. Many homes have solar panels. These panels collect the sun's energy and store it to use later. Many people use solar power to heat the water in their homes. **1** However, solar power is a little unreliable. **2** It depends upon the weather. **3** So in cloudy or rainy weather, people cannot use it. **4**

There are several other sources of renewable energy. However, water and the sun are the two most common.

---

renewable *adj* able to use again
hydroelectric *adj* using water power to produce electricity

1 According to paragraph 1, which of the following is true of oil and natural gas?
   - Ⓐ They are renewable sources of energy.
   - Ⓑ People use them only for cars and airplanes.
   - Ⓒ Someone discovered them in the twentieth century.
   - Ⓓ Their supply is running out.

2 According to paragraphs 2 and 3, which of the following is NOT true of renewable energy?
   - Ⓐ Water is a renewable resource.
   - Ⓑ People can use it again.
   - Ⓒ It is difficult to create.
   - Ⓓ It can come from the sun.

3 The word "collect" in the passage is closest in meaning to
   - Ⓐ gather
   - Ⓑ meet
   - Ⓒ move
   - Ⓓ change

4 The word "it" in the passage refers to
   - Ⓐ renewable energy
   - Ⓑ the water
   - Ⓒ solar power
   - Ⓓ the weather

5 Look at the four squares [■] that indicate where the following sentence could be added to the passage.

   On the other hand, people can use it in sunny areas every day.

   Where would the sentence best fit?

   Click on a square [■] to add the sentence to the passage.

Chapter ❽ 155

6 *Directions:* Complete the table below to summarize the information about energy. Match the appropriate statements to the type of energy it applies to. *This question is worth 3 points.*

Statements

1. There is only one kind of it.
2. People used it very much in the twentieth century.
3. People can use it again and again.
4. People can make it from the sun's power.
5. People can create it by using a dam.
6. There is a limited supply of it.
7. Planes and cars can use only this.

ENERGY

Oil and Gas	Renewable Energy
•	•
•	•
	•

Actual Test

Actual Test 1

Western Migration in the United States

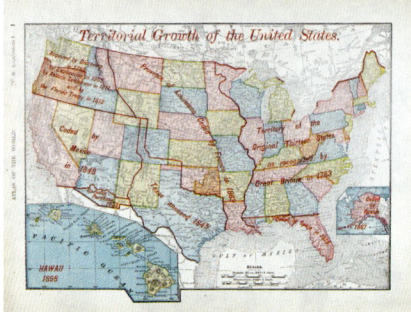

When the United States became a country, there were thirteen states. They were all by the east coast of North America. Over time, people began making their way west. This western migration took decades. But eventually, there were people living from the Atlantic coast to the Pacific coast.

1 In 1775, around two and a half million people lived in America. **2** This number steadily increased in the late 1700s and 1800s. **3** Most of the people came from Europe. **4** They wanted to have their own land. As a result, they began to head west.

At first, people moved toward the Great Lakes area. This covered land in the modern-day states of Ohio, Indiana, Illinois, and Michigan. People in the south also began to move west. By the 1800s, there were many settlements by the Mississippi River. It traveled down the country from the north to the south. Few people crossed the river though.

This changed in 1803. In that year, President Thomas Jefferson made the Louisiana Purchase from France. It was an enormous amount of land that almost doubled the size of the country. Slowly but steadily, people began heading west across the land. All throughout the 1800s, western migrations occurred. By 1890, there were forty-four states in the country. The government then declared that the west had been completely explored.

decade n a period lasting ten years
settlement n a small community of people

1. According to paragraph 1, which of the following is true of the United States?
   Ⓐ It was founded decades ago.
   Ⓑ It was located only on the Pacific coast.
   Ⓒ Its first states were on the coast.
   Ⓓ It has thirteen states today.

2. The word "head" in the passage is closest in meaning to
   Ⓐ travel
   Ⓑ look
   Ⓒ think about
   Ⓓ search for

3. In paragraph 2, which of the following can be inferred about America?
   Ⓐ It fought many wars in the 1800s.
   Ⓑ It was larger than Europe.
   Ⓒ Its population increased in the 1800s.
   Ⓓ It gave away land to people.

4. In paragraph 3, why does the author mention "the Great Lakes area"?
   Ⓐ To name all of the lakes there
   Ⓑ To point out its size
   Ⓒ To state where people moved
   Ⓓ To compare it with the south

5. In paragraph 3, the author's description of the Mississippi River mentions which of the following?
   Ⓐ How long it is
   Ⓑ What states it flows through
   Ⓒ Which direction is goes
   Ⓓ What settlements were by it

6 The word "It" in the passage refers to

- Ⓐ That year
- Ⓑ The Louisiana Purchase
- Ⓒ France
- Ⓓ The country

7 The word "steadily" in the passage is closest in meaning to

- Ⓐ constantly
- Ⓑ fairly
- Ⓒ clearly
- Ⓓ apparently

8 In paragraph 4, all of the following questions are answered EXCEPT:

- Ⓐ What did the government do in 1890?
- Ⓑ How large was the Louisiana Purchase?
- Ⓒ When was the Louisiana Purchase made?
- Ⓓ How much did the Louisiana Purchase cost?

9 Look at the four squares [■] that indicate where the following sentence could be added to the passage.

They left their homelands to start new lives in a new land.

Where would the sentence best fit?

Click on a square [■] to add the sentence to the passage.

10 *Directions*: An introductory sentence for a brief summary of the passage is provided below. Complete the summary by selecting the THREE answer choices that express the most important ideas in the passage. Some answer choices do not belong in the summary because they express ideas that are not presented in the passage or are minor ideas in the passage. *This question is worth 2 points.*

People moved west across the United States during the 1800s.

-
-
-

Answer Choices

1. Most people came to America from Europe.
2. It took decades for people to move west across North America.
3. People moved away from the Atlantic toward Great Lakes.
4. The Louisiana Purchase helped make people go west.
5. Many new states were formed out of the Louisiana Purchase.
6. There were thirteen states when the United States became a country.

Actual Test 2

Desertification

Deserts cover twenty percent of the Earth's land. There are deserts on every continent. In many places, the desert is expanding. This is called desertification. There are many reasons it can take place. It can happen due to the actions of nature and humans.

Desertification usually happens on arid or semiarid land. There are several steps in the process. First, many water sources dry up or vanish. This includes groundwater sources beneath the surface. The soil may become salty. So plants start to die. The wind may blow fertile topsoil away and leaves poor soil that cannot support plant life. Those events are all factors in creating new desert land.

One place where desertification is happening now is the Sahara Desert. It covers a huge part of northern Africa. It is also getting bigger each year. ■1 In some places, it moves south forty kilometers a year. ■2 This is not the only place where deserts are forming. ■3 It is also happening in other parts of Africa, Australia, Asia, and North America. ■4

In most cases, desertification happens naturally. Yet humans can contribute to it as well. By cutting down trees, people make the soil easier to erode. And when farmers use too much groundwater, that can dry up the land.

---

arid **adj** very dry
groundwater **n** water found beneath the Earth's surface

1 The word "expanding" in the passage is closest in meaning to
   Ⓐ forming
   Ⓑ removing
   Ⓒ growing
   Ⓓ harming

2 According to paragraph 1, which of the following is true of deserts?
   Ⓐ People cannot live in them.
   Ⓑ They are all around the Earth.
   Ⓒ Some are bigger than oceans.
   Ⓓ People can make them.

3 The word "vanish" is closest in meaning to
   Ⓐ disappear
   Ⓑ swell
   Ⓒ develop
   Ⓓ move

4 Which of the following best expresses the essential information in the highlighted sentence? *Incorrect* answer choices change the meaning in important ways or leave out essential information.
   Ⓐ The soil the wind blows away cannot support plants.
   Ⓑ Plants cannot live in places with heavy winds.
   Ⓒ The wind removes good soil and leaves bad soil.
   Ⓓ Poor soil is not good for plants to grow in.

5 According to paragraph 2, desertification happens
   Ⓐ slowly at first
   Ⓑ for several reasons
   Ⓒ only in hot places
   Ⓓ in summer months

Actual Test 163

6 The author discusses "the Sahara Desert" in paragraph 3 in order to

- Ⓐ argue that desertification is not a problem
- Ⓑ explain how desertification happens
- Ⓒ claim it will cover all of Africa soon
- Ⓓ show how desertification is affecting it

7 In paragraph 3, the author's description of the Sahara Desert mentions all of the following EXCEPT:

- Ⓐ What is happening to it
- Ⓑ How big it is getting
- Ⓒ Where it is located
- Ⓓ What countries it is in

8 In paragraphs 3 and 4, the author implies that desertification

- Ⓐ is making some deserts smaller
- Ⓑ is a problem in many places
- Ⓒ is only happening in Africa
- Ⓓ is killing people around the world

9 Look at the four squares [■] that indicate where the following sentence could be added to the passage.

It happens more slowly in other places there.

Where would the sentence best fit?

Click on a square [■] to add the sentence to the passage.

10 *Directions:* Complete the table below to summarize the information about desertification. Match the appropriate statements to the reason for desertification it applies to. *This question is worth 3 points.*

Statements

1. The wind can blow away soil.
2. People cut down trees.
3. The dirt becomes salty.
4. People build homes on land.
5. Rain stops falling in places.
6. There is less water under the ground.
7. Farmers use a lot of groundwater.

REASON FOR DESERTIFICATION

Nature	Humans
•	•
•	•
•	

Actual Test 3

Nikola Tesla

One of the most brilliant inventors in history was Nikola Tesla. He was born in 1856 and died in 1943. He did work in a number of different fields. He held more than 100 patents in the United States when he died. Many of his inventions were important. Some of his ideas also led to more modern-day inventions.

Most people know Tesla for his work on alternating current (AC). AC power lets electricity be sent long distances in an efficient manner. Tesla did not invent AC. But his work let its use spread far.

One of Tesla's dreams was to provide the world with energy without using wires. **1** In 1891, he invented the Tesla coil. **2** It was able to transmit electricity with no wires. **3** It was used in radio antennas and telegraphs at first. **4** It also later led to many other advances in the field of wireless technology.

Tesla contributed to the field of hydroelectric power, too. He designed a generator using AC power at Niagara Falls. It was a big success. A decade later, hydroelectric power created around ten percent of all power in the United States. Many power stations used Tesla's designs.

Those are just a few of his inventions. Even today, Tesla's work has a tremendous influence on the entire world.

patent **n** the right to make and sell an invention
hydroelectric power **n** power created from moving water

1 In paragraph 1, the author implies that Nikola Tesla
   Ⓐ died from a sickness
   Ⓑ was not from the United States
   Ⓒ became wealthy
   Ⓓ was a very smart man

2 According to paragraph 1, which of the following is NOT true of Nikola Tesla?
   Ⓐ He lived from 1856 to 1943.
   Ⓑ He had some important inventions.
   Ⓒ He predicted modern-day inventions.
   Ⓓ He did various kinds of work.

3 In paragraph 2, the author uses "alternating current" as an example of
   Ⓐ Tesla's most important invention
   Ⓑ the type of electricity people use today
   Ⓒ something that Tesla helped develop
   Ⓓ the best way to send electricity

4 The word "transmit" in the passage is closest in meaning to
   Ⓐ create
   Ⓑ store
   Ⓒ use
   Ⓓ send

5 The word "It" in the passage refers to
   Ⓐ The world
   Ⓑ Energy
   Ⓒ The Tesla coil
   Ⓓ Electricity

6 According to paragraph 3, which of the following is true of the Tesla coil?

- Ⓐ It led to the invention of the radio.
- Ⓑ It helped develop cellphones.
- Ⓒ It was used in some telegraphs.
- Ⓓ It sent electricity around the world.

7 According to paragraph 4, Tesla's work at Niagara Falls

- Ⓐ helped develop hydroelectric power
- Ⓑ provided electricity for ten percent of the United States
- Ⓒ took many years to complete
- Ⓓ made him a very rich man

8 The word "tremendous" in the passage is closest in meaning to

- Ⓐ great
- Ⓑ fast
- Ⓒ dangerous
- Ⓓ important

9 Look at the four squares [■] that indicate where the following sentence could be added to the passage.

This is known as wireless technology today.

Where would the sentence best fit?

Click on a square [■] to add the sentence to the passage.

10 *Directions:* An introductory sentence for a brief summary of the passage is provided below. Complete the summary by selecting the THREE answer choices that express the most important ideas in the passage. Some answer choices do not belong in the summary because they express ideas that are not presented in the passage or are minor ideas in the passage. *This question is worth 2 points.*

Nikola Tesla made many important inventions in his life.

-
-
-

Answer Choices

1 Tesla moved to the United States later in his life.	4 Tesla had more than 100 patents in the United States.
2 Many people remember the work that Tesla did.	5 The Tesla coil helped develop wireless technology.
3 Tesla's work on dams was used in other places later.	6 The AC power Tesla developed could send electricity far.

High Score iBT TOEFL READING For Junior Beginner
2nd Edition

Publisher Kyudo Chung
Editors Woonhee Park, Sangik Cho
Author Michael A. Putlack
Designers Minji Kim, Yeji Kim

First published in December 2007 by Happy House
Second edition first published in June 2023 by Darakwon, Inc.
Darakwon Bldg., 211, Munbal-ro, Paju-si, Gyeonggi-do 10881
Republic of Korea
Tel: 82-2-736-2031 (Ext. 250)
Fax: 82-2-732-2037

Copyright © 2007 Happy House, 2023 Darakwon

All rights reserved. No part of this publication may be reproduced, stored in a retrieval system, or transmitted in any form or by any means, electronic, mechanical, photocopying or otherwise, without the prior consent of the copyright owner. Refund after purchase is possible only according to the company regulations. Contact the above telephone number for any inquiries. Consumer damages caused by loss, damage, etc. can be compensated according to the consumer dispute resolution standards announced by the Korea Fair Trade Commission. An incorrectly collated book will be exchanged.

ISBN 978-89-277-8057-1 14740
978-89-277-8056-4 14740 (set)

www.darakwon.co.kr

Photo Credits
Shutterstock.com

Components Main Book / Answer Key
9 8 7 6 5 4 3   24 25 26 27 28

High Score

iBT TOEFL READING For Junior

2nd Edition

Beginner

Answer Key

High Score iBT TOEFL READING For Junior

Beginner

Answer Key

CHAPTER 1 History

Understanding TOEFL Question Types & Reading Skills p.14

1 Question Types ▶ Sample Question
ⓒ

해석 초창기 미국 탐험가들

일찍이 신세계로 탐험을 떠난 많은 모험가들이 있었다. 1513년, 폰세 데 레온은 플로리다로 갔다. 그는 금을 찾고 있었다. 에르난 코르테스는 1519년에 멕시코를 탐험했다. 그리고 1583년, 월터 롤리 경은 배로 버지니아에 상륙했다.

2 Reading Skills ▶ Check-Up
1 gold
2 Mexico
3 Walter Raleigh

• Exercise 1 • p.16

정답 ⓓ

해석 에드먼드 힐러리 경

에베레스트산은 세계에서 가장 높은 산이다. 과거에 많은 사람들이 그 산을 오르기 위해 노력했다. 그러나 그들은 실패했다. 하지만 두 사람은 실패하지 않았다. 한 사람은 에드먼드 힐러리 경이었다. 그는 뉴질랜드 사람이었다. 다른 한 사람은 그의 셰르파족 안내인 텐징 노르가이였다. 1953년 5월 29일, 그들은 에베레스트산을 올랐다. 그 이후 힐러리는 아주 유명해졌다. 후에, 그는 히말라야 산맥의 다른 봉우리들을 1956년에 등반했다.

Reading Skills

1 May 29, 1953
2 1956

• Exercise 2 • p.17

정답 ⓒ

해석 중국의 만리장성

중국 제국에는 많은 적들이 있었다. 그들은 종종 중국을 침범했고 그곳에 사는 사람들을 공격했다. 그래서 중국인들은 긴 벽을 건설했다. 그들은 기원전 400년경에 그것을 세우기 시작했다. 그들은 16세기에 완성했다. 그들은 그것을 만리장성이라 불렀다. 그 벽은 거의 4,000마일에 걸쳐져 있다. 중국인들은 그 벽에 군사들을 배치했다. 그들은 외세의 침입으로부터 중국을 보호했다.

Reading Skills

1 400 B.C.
2 sixteenth(16th)

• Exercise 3 • p.18

정답 ⓐ

해석 남북전쟁

19세기에 미국에는 많은 문제들이 있었다. 북부와 남부는 매우 달랐다. 많은 남부인들이 노예를 소유하고 있었다. 그러나 대부분의 북부인들은 그렇지 않았다. 북부에는 공장이 있었다. 남부는 대부분 농장이었다. 이후에, 두 지역 사이에는 다툼이 많았다. 그들은 그 문제들을 해결할 수 없었다. 결국 1861년 4월 12일, 전쟁이 시작되었다. 이후인 1865년에 북부가 남북전쟁에서 승리했다.

Reading Skills

1 April 12, 1861
2 1865

• Exercise 4 • p.19

정답 ⓓ

해석 율리우스 카이사르

율리우스 카이사르는 로마의 위대한 장군이었다. 그는 기원전 100년경에 태어났다. 후에, 그는 자신의 군대를 이끌고 갈리아를 정복했다. 그런 다음, 그는 로마의 독재자가 되었다. 카이사르는 많은 개혁을 했다. 그는 로마인들의 사회적, 정치적 삶을 변화시켰다. 그러나 많은 로마인들이 그를 싫어했다. 그래서 기원전 44년, 일부 원로원들이 그를 암살했다. 안타깝게도 카이사르는 자신의 개혁을 완수하지 못했다.

Reading Skills

4, 2, 3, 1

• Exercise 5 • p.20

정답 Q1 ⓑ Q2 ⓑ

해석 왕들의 계곡

기원전 16세기부터, 이집트인들은 파라오와 다른 귀족들을 이집트의 한 지역에 매장하기 시작했다. 그들은 이 지역을 '왕들의 계곡'이라고 불렀다. 기원전 11세기까지 그들은 그 계곡에 왕족의 무덤을 만들었다. 이집트인들은 사후세계를 믿었다. 그래서 그들은 죽은 사람이 편안하기를 원했다. 이러한 이유로 그들은 왕의 무덤에 여러 가지 많은 보물들을 넣었다.

고고학자인 하워드 카터는 종종 그 계곡에서 무덤들을 찾아다녔다. 1922년에 그는 투탕카멘 왕의 무덤을 발견했다. 사람들은 보통 그를 투트 왕이라고 부른다. 그 무덤에는 금과 보석이 많이 있었다. 무덤 도굴꾼들이 보물을 훔쳐간 적이 없었다. 많은 박물관들이 투트 왕의 전시회를 열고 있다. 가장 유명한 것은 1972년에 열린 전시회였다.

Reading Skills

1 pharaohs and other nobles
2 Tutankhamen
3 1972

• Exercise 6 •
p.21

정답 Q1 ⓒ Q2 Ⓐ

해석 　　　　워싱턴이 델라웨어강을 건너다

미국 독립 혁명은 1775년에 어렵게 시작되었다. 초반의 몇 달은 아주 힘들었다. 처음에 많은 식민지 개척자들이 그 전쟁을 포기하고 싶어 했다. 1776년 겨울 동안 조지 워싱턴 장군은 한 가지 아이디어를 생각해냈다. 그는 위대한 전투에서 이기고 싶었다. 그는 그것이 미국 군인들에게 용기를 줄 것이라고 믿었다.

1776년 12월 25일 크리스마스 밤이었다. 워싱턴은 2,400명의 병사를 이끌고 델라웨어강을 건넜다. 그는 1,500명의 독일 군대를 공격하려 했다. 그들은 영국군을 위해서 싸우고 있었다. 미국군은 조용히 배를 타고 강을 건넜다. 독일군은 그들을 발견하지 못했다. 전투가 시작되었다. 그것은 빨리 끝났다. 한 시간 반 후에 독일군은 항복했다. 이 승리로 미국군은 전쟁을 계속할 수 있게 되었다. 그리고 1781년에 그들은 전쟁에서 승리했다.

Reading Skills

1　1775
2　December 25, 1776
3　1781

• Exercise 7 •
p.22

정답 Q1 ⓒ Q2 Ⓐ

해석 　　　　아테네의 민주주의

고대에는 대부분의 지역에 왕이 있었다. 그 왕들이 영토를 지배했다. 그러나 한 지역은 달랐다. 아테네는 그리스의 도시국가였다. 그곳의 사람들은 민주주의 체제하에서 살았다. 그러나 아테네의 민주주의에서는 성인 남성인 시민들만이 투표를 할 수 있었다. 그래서 그것은 진정한 의미의 민주주의는 아니었다. 그렇다고 해도 다른 곳들에 비해서는 더 나았다. 많은 사람들이 아테네의 민주주의를 만들었다. 아테네의 남성들은 모두 아테네가 취해야 할 행동들을 결정하는 데 일조했다.

첫 번째로, 솔론은 기원전 594년경에 민주주의의 발전을 도왔다. 그는 처음으로 개혁을 이룬 사람이었다. 그러나 다른 많은 위대한 지도자들이 있었다. 클레이스테네스는 기원전 508년에 민주주의를 확장시켰다. 페리클레스는 가장 위대한 아테네인이었다. 그는 기원전 461년부터 429년경까지 아테네를 이끌었다. 유감스럽게도, 아테네는 민주주의를 유지하지 못했다. 기원전 322년에 마케도니아인들이 그곳의 민주주의를 종식시켰다.

Reading Skills

1　Solon
2　508 B.C.
3　Pericles
4　Macedonians

• Exercise 8 •
p.23

정답 Q1 ⓒ Q2 Ⓑ

해석 　　　　비잔틴 제국

비잔틴 제국은 4세기에 세워졌다. 수도는 콘스탄티노플이었다. 그곳은 오늘날 튀르키예의 이스탄불이라는 도시이다. 제국은 한때 매우 강력했다. 또한 광범위한 영토를 통치했다. 비잔틴 제국은 유럽의 남동부와 튀르키예의 상당 부분을 통치했다. 다른 유럽 지역과 아프리카, 중동 지방 또한 통치했다.

제국은 1,000년 이상 지속되었다. 위대한 통치자들이 많았다. 첫 번째는 콘스탄티누스 대제였다. 이후에는 유스티니아누스 대제가 황제가 되었다. 그는 527년부터 565년까지 통치를 했다. 오랜 기간 동안 제국은 외부의 침략으로부터 유럽을 지켰다. 하지만 투르크족이 매우 강력해졌다. 여러 해의 전쟁을 거친 후 그들은 수도를 점령했다. 그에 따라 비잔틴 제국은 멸망했다. 1453년에 일어난 일이었다.

Reading Skills

2, 4, 1, 3

Grammar Point
p.24

◉ Grammar Check-Up

Ⓐ **Proper Nouns:** Egypt, Solon, America, Civil War, Athens, Chinese
Common Nouns: building, river, archaeologist, democracy, general, tomb, capital, people, mountain

Ⓑ Soviet Union, rockets, space, Apollo, moon

Ⓒ 1 ☐ Put some sugars in the iced tea.
2 ☑ I have ten fingers and ten toes.
3 ☐ There are too many car on the road.
4 ☑ He is putting on his shoes now.
5 ☑ The air in the city is very dirty.
6 ☐ We saw some deers in the forest.

Ⓓ 1 fish
2 a pencil
3 snow
4 soda
5 automobiles

Vocabulary Review
p.26

Ⓐ 1 highest
2 Archaeologists
3 pharaohs
4 vote
5 sailed

Ⓑ 1 ⓒ 2 Ⓐ 3 Ⓓ 4 ⓒ 5 Ⓑ

Ⓒ 1 Ⓑ 2 Ⓐ 3 ⓒ 4 Ⓐ 5 Ⓓ

Ⓓ 1 robbers
2 expand
3 invaders
4 battle
5 slave

Practice Test   p.28

1 ⓒ   2 ⓓ   3 ⓑ   4 ⓓ   5 ⓐ   6 ②, ⑤, ⑥

해석   조지 워싱턴

조지 워싱턴은 미국 역사상 가장 위대한 미국인 중 한 사람이었다. 그는 일생 동안 많은 일을 이루어냈다. 그는 성공한 농부였다. 그는 정치가였다. 그는 독립전쟁에서 대영제국을 상대로 미국군을 승리로 이끌었다. 그는 또한 미국의 초대 대통령이었다.

대통령으로서 워싱턴은 국가의 후임 지도자들을 위한 많은 선례들을 세우는 데 일조했다. 이러한 선례들은 매우 중요했다. 그래서 다른 사람들도 보통 워싱턴의 선례들을 따랐다.

많은 초기의 미국인들은 왕을 경멸했다. 그들은 미국도 군주제 국가가 될까 봐 두려워했다. 그럼에도 많은 미국인들은 워싱턴이 왕이 되기를 원했다. 그러나 그는 왕이 되는 것을 거부했다. 대신에 그는 대통령으로서 두 번의 임기를 연임했을 뿐이었다. 그러고나서 그는 퇴임했다. 약 150년 동안 다른 모든 대통령들이 그의 선례를 따랐다. 그들은 한 번 혹은 두 번의 임기 동안만 역임했다. 두 번 이상 연임한 유일한 사람은 프랭클린 D. 루즈벨트였다. 그는 1932년부터 1945년까지 대통령을 역임했다.

워싱턴은 또한 국가가 다른 국가의 일에 관여하는 데 신중해야 한다고 경고했다. 미국은 많은 전쟁을 치렀다. 그러나 많은 미국인들이 고립주의를 원한다. 그들은 정말로 다른 국가의 일에 신경 쓰지 않는다. 몇몇 대통령들 또한 워싱턴의 선례를 따랐다. 이런 식으로, 워싱턴은 역대 가장 영향력 있는 미국 대통령들 중 한 사람이었다.

CHAPTER 2 Geography

Understanding TOEFL Question Types & Reading Skills   p.32

1 Question Types ▶ Sample Question

ⓓ

해석   계곡

계곡은 저지대이다. 빙하계곡과 강계곡이 있다. 빙하계곡은 천천히 움직이는 얼음으로 인해 형성된다. 그러나 강계곡은 유수로 인해 형성된다. 강계곡은 빙하계곡에 비해 더 빠르게 형성된다. 빙하계곡의 바닥은 폭이 넓다. 그러나 강계곡의 바닥은 폭이 좁다.

2 Reading Skills ▶ Check-Up

ⓒ

• Exercise 1 •   p.34

정답 ⓐ

해석   거대한 강

나일강과 아마존강은 세계의 거대한 두 강이다. 그 강들은 세계에서 가장 크다. 그러나 나일강이 아마존강보다 더 길다. 그 강은 아프리카에 있다. 아마존강은 남아메리카 대륙에 있다. 두 강 모두 높은 산에서 시작된다. 나일강은 사막을 통과하여 남쪽에서 북쪽으로 흐른다. 반면에 아마존강은 열대 우림을 통과하여 서쪽에서 동쪽으로 흐른다.

Reading Skills

S, D, D, S

• Exercise 2 •   p.35

정답 ⓒ

해석   오스트레일리아와 그린란드

오스트레일리아와 그린란드는 거대한 두 개의 땅덩어리이다. 어떤 사람들은 오스트레일리아가 지구상에서 가장 큰 섬이라고 생각한다. 그러나 그렇지 않다. 그것은 섬이 아니다. 그것은 대륙이다. 그것은 그린란드가 세계에서 가장 큰 섬이라는 것을 의미한다. 오스트레일리아에는 많은 사람들이 산다. 그러나 그린란드에는 사람이 거의 살지 않는다. 그린란드의 날씨는 보통 춥다. 그러나 오스트레일리아의 날씨는 훨씬 더 따뜻하다.

Reading Skills

ⓓ

• Exercise 3 •   p.36

정답 ⓐ

해석   개천과 도랑

개천과 도랑은 둘 다 물의 흐름의 형태이다. 사람들은 종종 개천과 도랑이 똑같다고 생각한다. 그러나 실제로는 다르다. 개천이 도랑보다 더 길다. 또한 개천에는 도랑보다 더 많은 양의 물이 흐른다. 도랑에는 물이 없는 경우도 있다. 그러나 개천에는 항상 물이 흐르고 있다. 마지막으로, 개천에서는 배를 운행할 수 있다. 그러나 도랑에서는 배를 이용할 수 없다.

Reading Skills

D, S, D, D

• Exercise 4 •   p.37

정답 ⓑ

해석   협곡

협곡은 좁고 깊은 계곡이다. 그것은 강에 의해 형성된다. 오랜 기간에 걸쳐 흐르는 물이 땅을 침식시킨다. 이로써 협곡이 만들어진다. 대부분의 협곡에는 매우 가파른 벽이 있다. 그랜드 캐니언과 같은 일부 계곡의 경우 그 깊이가 수천 피트가 될 수 있다. 모든 협곡이 땅에 있는 것은 아니다. 어떤 협곡은 물속에 있다. 이러한 협곡 역시 물의 침식 작용에 의해 형성된다.

Reading Skills

ⓑ

• Exercise 5 •   p.38

정답 Q1 ⓓ   Q2 ⓒ

해석   지구의 극점

남극과 북극은 지구의 반대편 끝에 있다. 두 지역 모두 극도로 격리되어 있고 매우 춥다. 그러나 남극이 북극보다 더 추워질 수 있다. 북극은 지구의 최북단 지역이다. 그것은 북극대륙에 위치해 있다. 반면에 남극은 지구의 최남단 지역이다. 그것은 남극대륙에 위치해 있다.

북극은 실제로 북극해의 중간지점에 있다. 그러나 남극은 땅 위에 있다. 두 극지방에는 모두 어마어마한 양의 얼음이 있다. 그러나 남극에 있는 얼음이 북극에 있는 얼음보다 더 두껍다.

오랜 시간 동안 사람들은 두 극점에 도달하기를 꿈꿨다. 마침내 한 탐험대가 남극에 앞서 북극에 먼저 도착했다.

Reading Skills

D, D, S, S

• Exercise 6 •   p.39

정답   Q1 ⓑ   Q2 ⓒ

해석   사막

어떤 사람들은 모든 사막이 뜨겁다고 여긴다. 그러나 그렇지 않다. 지구에는 차가운 사막도 몇 군데 있다. 아프리카에 있는 사하라 사막은 뜨거운 사막의 전형이다. 남극대륙은 세계에서 가장 크고 추운 사막이다. 실제로 남극은 사하라 사막보다 더 크다. 사실, 그것은 거대한 대륙이다.

사하라 사막은 대륙의 일부에 불과하다. 그곳에는 모래가 많고 바람이 많이 분다. 그러나 남극의 차가운 사막들에는 눈과 얼음이 많다. 사하라 사막은 지구상에서 가장 더운 지역이다. 남극은 세계에서 가장 추운 지역이다. 마지막으로, 남극에는 물의 형태가 전혀 없다. 그러나 사하라 사막에는 물이 있다. 이러한 물의 형태가 오아시스이다.

Reading Skills

ⓓ

• Exercise 7 •   p.40

정답   Q1 ⓓ   Q2 ⓒ

해석   산맥

유명한 두 산맥으로는 히말라야 산맥과 애팔래치아 산맥이 있다. 흥미롭게도 두 산맥은 서로 매우 다르다.

히말라야 산맥 대부분은 아시아의 네팔에 위치해 있다. 그러나 중국과 인도와 같은 다른 나라에도 걸쳐져 있다. 히말라야 산맥에는 세계에서 가장 높은 산봉우리들이 있다. 그 봉우리들은 약 7000만년 전에 형성되었다. 그리고 그 봉우리들은 여전히 성장하고 있다.

애팔래치아 산맥은 미국에 있다. 애팔래치아 산맥은 히말라야 산맥만큼 높거나 위험하지 않다. 사실 그 산맥의 봉우리들은 꽤 낮다. 그래서 그 봉우리들을 오르기가 쉽다. 이 점이 히말라야 산맥과 매우 다른 점이다. 애팔래치아 산맥은 약 3억년 전에 형성되었다. 그러니까 애팔래치아 산맥이 히말라야 산맥보다 훨씬 더 오래된 것이다. 애팔래치아 산맥은 오래 전에 성장을 멈추었다.

Reading Skills

S, D, S, D

• Exercise 8 •   p.41

정답   Q1 ⓒ   Q2 ⓑ

해석   한국과 일본

한국과 일본은 둘 다 북동아시아에 있는 국가이다. 그러나 두 나라는 서로 다른 부분들이 있다. 예를 들면, 한국은 반도이다. 그래서 바다가 삼면을 감싸고 있다. 그러나 일본은 섬나라이다. 일본에는 4개의 큰 섬이 있다. 또한 작은 섬들도 많다. 한국에도 많은 섬들이 있다.

얼핏 보기에 두 나라는 서로 매우 다른 것처럼 보인다. 그러나 실제로는 서로 비슷하다. 두 나라 모두 기후가 유사하다. 그래서 종종 같은 종류의 날씨를 겪는다. 두 나라 모두 여름이 끝날 무렵에 태풍을 겪는다. 그렇지만 태풍은 대체로 일본에서 더 강력하다. 두 나라 모두 광대한 산맥이 있다. 그러나 일본에 가장 높은 산이 있다. 그것은 후지산이다. 그러니까, 두 나라는 여러 가지 면에서 상당히 비슷하다.

Reading Skills

ⓑ

Grammar Point   p.42

Grammar Check-Up

A   1   pleased with
     2   surprised at
     3   afraid of
     4   different from
     5   concerned about

B   1 ⓒ   2 ⓓ   3 ⓒ   4 ⓓ   5 ⓑ

C   1 ⓒ   2 ⓐ   3 ⓓ

Vocabulary Review   p.44

A   1   accurate
     2   longer
     3   climate
     4   desert
     5   continents

B   1 ⓒ   2 ⓑ   3 ⓓ   4 ⓐ   5 ⓑ

C   1 ⓓ   2 ⓑ   3 ⓐ   4 ⓓ   5 ⓐ

D   1   surrounds
     2   narrow
     3   incorrect
     4   stream
     5   landmass

Practice Test   p.46

1 Ⓓ   2 Ⓐ   3 Ⓓ   4 Ⓒ   5 ▣   6 ①, ③, ⑤

해석   툰드라

툰드라는 극도로 추운 날씨를 겪는 지역에서만 찾아볼 수 있는 생물군계의 한 유형이다. 툰드라는 두 가지 주요한 특징을 가지고 있다. 첫 번째는 그 지역에 얼어붙은 땅이 있어야 한다는 점이다. 두 번째는 그곳에 키가 큰 나무가 없다는 점이다.

지구 표면의 상당 부분인 20퍼센트 정도가 툰드라이다. 툰드라는 평지일 수도 있지만, 산과 언덕을 포함할 수도 있다. 러시아, 캐나다, 그린란드, 북유럽, 그리고 알래스카의 많은 곳이 툰드라로 여겨진다. 그 지역에 있는 땅은 북극 툰드라라고 불린다. (또 다른 종류로는 알파인 툰드라가 있으며, 그것은 산악 지대에서 발견된다.) 북극 툰드라는 1년 내내 날씨가 춥다. 그 결과 표토 바로 밑의 땅이 항상 얼어 있다. 이는 영구동토층으로 알려져 있다. 어떤 곳에서는 영구동토층의 깊이가 450미터 이상에 이를 수도 있다.

하층토가 얼어 있기 때문에 툰드라에서는 나무가 살지 못한다. 나무의 뿌리가 땅속 깊은 곳까지 자랄 수 없는 것이다. 툰드라에 사는 식물 대다수는 이끼와 관목이다. 어떤 곳에서는 야생초가 자라기도 한다. 이러한 식물들은 모두 지면에서 높지 않은 높이까지 자란다. 그리고 땅속 깊은 곳까지 뿌리를 내릴 필요가 없다.

CHAPTER 3 Technology

Understanding TOEFL Question Types & Reading Skills   p.50

① Question Types ▶ Sample Question

Ⓒ

해석   조립라인

사람들은 느린 속도로 제품을 제작하곤 했다. 한 사람이 한 제품의 모든 부속품들을 만들었다. 그러나 헨리 포드는 아이디어를 생각해 냈다. 그는 조립라인을 사용했다. 일꾼들은 제조 과정 중 어느 한 부분에 전문화되었다. 그래서 여러 가지 제품에 대한 제작이 훨씬 더 빨라졌다.

② Reading Skills ▶ Check-Up

E, C

• Exercise 1 •   p.52

정답 Ⓓ

해석   인터넷

인터넷은 최근 60여년 동안에 가장 중요한 발명 중의 하나였다. 1960년대에 미국군이 인터넷을 직접 만들기 시작했다. 그들은 핵전쟁에 대해 걱정했다. 그래서 그들은 사람들과 접촉할 안전한 방법을 원했다. 다른 조직들은 인터넷을 많이 개선시켜 왔다. 그러한 발전 덕분에, 수백만 명의 사람들이 매일 인터넷을 사용하고 있다.

Reading Skills

1 C, E   2 E, C

• Exercise 2 •   p.53

정답 Ⓑ

해석   하늘을 나는 자동차

사람들은 항상 미래에 대해 생각한다. 그들은 다양한 발명품들을 개선하고 싶어 한다. 그래서 오늘날 많은 발명가들이 하늘을 나는 자동차에 대해 연구하고 있다. 실제로 이미 하늘을 나는 자동차가 어느 정도 있다. 그러나 지금 그것들은 너무 비싸다. 또한 너무 많은 연료를 사용한다. 그러나 언젠가 그것들은 상용화될 것이다. 그래서 많은 사람들이 하늘을 나는 자동차를 소유하게 될 것이다.

Reading Skills

1 E, C   2 C, E

• Exercise 3 •   p.54

정답 Ⓑ

해석   전신기

1800년대 중반에 사무엘 모스가 전신기를 발명했다. 전신기는 전기를 사용했다. 전신기는 전선을 통해 메시지를 보낼 수가 있었다. 이는 사람들이 소통하는 방식을 크게 변화시켰다. 그 전에는 사람들이 편지를 보냈다. 편지는 배달되기까지 오랜 시간이 걸렸다. 하지만 전신 메시지는 빠르게 받아 보았다. 따라서 사람들은 즉각적으로 이야기를 나눌 수 있었다. 전신기는 큰 인기를 얻었다. 사람들은 심지어 바다 건너편으로 메시지를 보낼 수 있었다. 이로써 사람들은 보다 더 가까워졌다.

Reading Skills

1 E, C   2 C, E

• Exercise 4 •   p.55

정답 Ⓐ

해석   콩코드 비행기

라이트 형제가 그들의 첫 비행기로 비행한 이후로 사람들은 항공사를 세우기 시작했다. 하늘을 나는 것은 운전을 하거나 기차를 타는 것보다 훨씬 더 빨랐다. 배로 대서양을 건너가는 것은 특히 시간이 많이 걸렸다. 그래서 영국과 프랑스의 기업들은 콩코드 비행기를 개발했다. 콩코드 비행기는 음속보다 더 빠르게 비행했다. 그 결과 사람들은 6시간이 아니라 3시간 만에 미국에서 영국으로 대서양을 건너갈 수 있게 되었다.

Reading Skills

1 E, C   2 C, E

• Exercise 5 •   p.56

정답 Q1 Ⓒ   Q2 Ⓑ

해석 　　　　　　　　　**산업혁명**

수세기 동안, 인류는 발명품을 거의 만들지 않았다. 그러나 18세기, 인류는 갑자기 많은 새로운 기계들을 만들기 시작했다. 사람들은 이 시대를 산업혁명기라고 부른다. 그것은 18세기 중반경에 시작되었다. 그리고 어떤 사람들은 그것이 여전히 진행 중이라고 믿는다.

섬유산업에서 많은 발전이 있었다. 리차드 아크라이트는 목화에서 실을 잣는 새로운 방식을 발명했다. 이것은 이전의 방식보다 더 빠르고 효율적이었다. 이 때문에 옷 가격이 훨씬 더 저렴해지게 되었다. 제임스 와트는 또한 증기기관을 발명했다. 그의 발명 덕분에, 사람들은 더 좋은 배를 만들 수 있었다. 사람들은 또한 그의 엔진으로 운행되는 기차를 고안했다. 사람들은 또한 쇠를 만드는 더 나은 방법을 만들어냈다. 이로 인해 쇠가 더 단단해졌다. 그래서 건물의 내구성이 훨씬 더 높아졌다.

Reading Skills
Ⓓ

• **Exercise 6** • ─────────────── p.57

정답 Q1 Ⓐ　Q2 Ⓒ

해석 　　　　　　　　　**인공위성**

1957년 소련 연방은 *스푸트니크*를 쏘아 올렸다. 이것이 세계 최초의 인공위성이었다. 그것은 잠깐 동안 궤도에 머물렀을 뿐이었다. 그렇지만 사람들은 인공위성이 매우 중요할 수 있다는 것을 깨달았다. 그 결과 지금은 수백 개의 인공위성이 지구의 궤도를 돌고 있다. 정부, 군대, 기업들이 인공위성을 우주로 보낸다. 그들은 여러 가지 이유로 자신의 이익에 따라 그렇게 하고 있다.

어떤 인공위성들은 날씨를 관측한다. 그것들은 지구의 많은 부분을 볼 수 있다. 그래서 날씨를 매우 잘 예측할 수 있다. 기후 패턴의 여러 변화들 또한 관측할 수 있다. 어떤 인공위성들은 통신에 도움을 준다. 그것들은 전화와 인터넷 연결을 도와준다. 그래서 사람들은 값싸고 편리하게 서로 연락할 수 있다. 그리고 또 다른 인공위성들은 국가를 감찰한다. 군대에서 이러한 것들을 사용한다. 그래서 그들은 다른 국가들의 군대를 감시할 수 있다.

Reading Skills
Ⓐ

• **Exercise 7** • ─────────────── p.58

정답 Q1 Ⓑ　Q2 Ⓓ

해석 　　　　　　　　　**구텐베르크와 인쇄기**

대부분의 역사 동안, 글을 읽을 수 있는 사람은 거의 없었다. 책은 매우 귀했다. 책은 대단히 비싼데다 만들려면 몇 달 혹은 몇 년이 걸렸다. 그러나 어떤 한 사람이 책을 누구나 이용할 수 있도록 만들었다.

요하네스 구텐베르크는 15세기에 독일에서 살았다. 그는 인쇄업자이자 금세공인이었다. 그는 책이 만들기 어렵다는 것을 깨달았다. 그래서 그는 활자를 만들었다. 이 과정 덕분에 사람들은 책을 빨리 만들 수 있었다. 그로 인해 책이 저렴해졌다.

구텐베르크의 인쇄기는 전 유럽에 퍼졌다. 곧, 사람들이 책을 수백 권씩 찍어냈다. 그 결과 더 많은 사람들이 이렇게 저렴한 책을 살 수 있었다. 사람들은 읽는 법도 배웠다. 그로 인해 유럽의 지식이 발전했다. 인쇄기 덕택에 유럽 전역에서 지식의 재탄생이 이루어졌다. 사람들은 이 시기를 르네상스 시대라고 불렀다.

Reading Skills
Ⓐ

• **Exercise 8** • ─────────────── p.59

정답 Q1 Ⓒ　Q2 Ⓓ

해석 　　　　　　　　　**토마스 에디슨**

역사상 가장 위대한 발명가 중의 한 사람은 토마스 에디슨이었다. 재미있게도, 처음에 사람들은 그가 우둔하다고 생각했다. 그는 학교를 3개월 동안만 다녔다. 그러나 에디슨은 열심히 노력했다. 그 결과, 그는 많은 위대한 업적들을 이루었다.

에디슨은 1,000여 건 이상의 발명품에 대해 특허를 얻었다. 그의 초기 발명품들 중 하나는 축음기였다. 이 기계는 사람들을 깜짝 놀라게 했다. 그것은 소리와 음악을 재생할 수 있었다.

그러나 에디슨의 가장 유명한 발명품은 전구였다. 사실 그가 최초의 전구를 발명한 것은 아니었다. 그는 처음으로 상용 가능한 전구를 발명했다. 전구 덕택에 사람들의 삶은 바뀌었다. 그들은 늦게까지 깨어 있었다. 그들은 야간 활동을 더 많이 할 수 있었다. 그들은 또한 가스나 장작에 의존해 불을 켤 필요가 없어졌다.

Reading Skills
Ⓒ

Grammar Point　　　　　　　　　　　p.60

Grammar Check-Up

Ⓐ　1　me
　　2　herself
　　3　He
　　4　yours
　　5　them

Ⓑ　1　ⓓ　2　ⓑ　3　ⓒ　4　ⓑ　5　ⓓ

Ⓒ　my, They, them, one after the other, It, beside themselves, All the same

Vocabulary Review　　　　　　　　　p.62

Ⓐ　1　orbits
　　2　connection
　　3　knowledge
　　4　satellites
　　5　inventions

Ⓑ　1　Ⓓ　2　Ⓑ　3　Ⓒ　4　Ⓒ　5　Ⓐ

Ⓒ　1　Ⓐ　2　Ⓐ　3　Ⓒ　4　Ⓓ　5　Ⓑ

D
1 enabled
2 specializes
3 launch
4 spinning
5 future

Practice Test p.64

1 ⓓ 2 ⓒ 3 ⓑ 4 ⓓ 5 ⓐ
6 Technological: 1, 5, 6 Medical: 3, 7

해석 우주 프로그램의 혜택

많은 미국인들이 우주 프로그램에 반감을 가지고 있다. 그들은 정부가 지구에 사는 사람들을 위해 더 많은 돈을 써야 한다고 생각한다. 그들은 우주 프로그램에서 얻는 혜택이 거의 없다고 주장한다. 그러나 정말로 그렇지 않다. 우주 프로그램은 실제로 여러 면에서 사람들에게 도움을 주고 있다.

첫째로, 천문학자들은 달, 행성, 태양계, 별에 대해 많은 것들을 알아내고 있다. 그래서 인류의 기본적인 지식이 발전하고 있다. 또한 많은 인공위성들이 행성이나 다른 은하계에 대한 정보를 지구로 보내고 있다. 이러한 것들이 우주 프로그램에서 얻는 혜택들이다.

두 번째로, 우주 프로그램은 일반적인 사람들의 삶에도 영향을 미치고 있다. 이것은 과학자들이 이루고 있는 기술적 진보 덕분이다. 무엇보다도 인공위성은 사람들이 케이블 TV를 보고 휴대폰을 사용하게 해 준다. 인공위성은 심지어 날씨를 예측하는 데 도움을 줄 수 있다. 또한 우주 프로그램에 종사하는 과학자들은 최초로 무선 기술을 개발했다. 그래서 오늘날 많은 여러 종류의 장비들이 전선을 쓰지 않는다.

게다가 의료 분야가 발전하고 있다. 예를 들어 많은 사람들이 레이저 수술을 받는다. 우주 프로그램에 종사하는 과학자들이 이 기술을 처음으로 발전시켰다. 심지어 CT 촬영과 MRI와 같은 신체 영상 촬영도 우주 분야의 발전에서 비롯되었다.

확실히 우주 프로그램은 많은 사람들에게 혜택을 주고 있다. 그것은 단지 과학자나 비행사들에게만 도움이 되는 것이 아니다. 오히려, 일반적인 사람들에게도 도움이 되고 있다.

CHAPTER 4 Education

Understanding TOEFL Question Types & Reading Skills p.68

1 Question Types ▶ Sample Question
ⓑ

해석 학습 교구

교사들은 수업시간에 많은 종류의 교구들을 사용한다. 먼저, 그들은 일반적인 교구들을 많이 가지고 있다. 이러한 것들에는 칠판, 유인물, 빔 프로젝터가 있다. 그들은 온라인 교구도 사용한다. 이러한 교구들로는 웹사이트, 인터넷 신문, 온라인 동영상 등이 있다.

2 Reading Skills ▶ Check-Up
ⓓ

• Exercise 1 • p.70

정답 ⓒ

해석 미국의 공립 및 사립 학교

미국에는 많은 유명한 대학들이 있다. 그 대학들 중 일부는 공립 학교들이다. 정부가 이러한 학교들을 지원한다. 노스캐롤라이나 대학교, 텍사스 대학교, UCLA가 몇몇 유명한 공립 학교들이다. 다른 유명한 대학들로는 사립 학교들이 있다. 개인이나 단체, 기관에서 이러한 학교들을 소유하고 있다. 듀크, 다트머스, 프린스턴이 몇몇 유명한 사립 학교들이다.

Reading Skills
ⓐ

• Exercise 2 • p.71

정답 ⓐ

해석 프리드리히 프뢰벨

과거에는 대부분의 영유아들이 학교에 다니지 않았다. 대신에 집에 머물면서 학습했다. 한 사람이 이것을 바꾸고 싶어 했다. 그의 이름은 프리드리히 프뢰벨이었다. 그는 영유아들을 위한 학교를 만들었다. 이 학교는 이후에 유치원이라고 불리게 되었다. 그는 학습에 있어서 놀이가 중요하다고 생각했다. 그는 또한 미술, 자연, 수학이 중요하다고 믿었다. 그의 생각은 큰 인기를 얻게 되었다. 그래서 1800년대에 많은 유치원들이 생겨났다.

Reading Skills
ⓓ

• Exercise 3 • p.72

정답 ⓑ

해석 대학의 학부

많은 대학들에는 최소 두 개의 다른 학부가 있다. 이 학부들에는 다양한 과가 있다. 대부분의 대학에 문리대가 있다. 다른 많은 대학에 공과대가 있다. 문리대에는 많은 전공과들이 있다. 역사, 철학, 문학이 있을 수 있다. 공과대에도 또한 여러 전공과가 있다. 이들 중에는 토목공학, 화학공학, 전기공학이 있다.

Reading Skills
ⓓ

• Exercise 4 • p.73

정답 ⓐ

해석 엘리트 대학

미국에는 많은 우수한 대학들이 있다. 많은 학생들이 그러한 대학에 입학하기를 꿈꾼다. 미국에서 아이비리그의 모든 학교들은 특히 우수하다. 4대 아이비리그 대학들은 예일, 하버드, 코넬, 콜롬비아 대학이다. 그 외 다른 훌륭한 미국

학교들이 많이 있다. MIT, 스탠포드, 미시간, UC 버클리는 모두 일류 학교들이다. 그곳에는 아주 뛰어난 교수와 학생 들이 있다.

Reading Skills
ⓒ

• **Exercise 5** • ——————————————— p.74

정답 Q1 Ⓑ   Q2 Ⓓ

해석   **최초의 서양 대학**

많은 사람들이 대학이 최근에 생겼다고 생각한다. 그러나 그렇지 않다. 서양에서 최초의 대학은 9세기에 등장했다. 바로 살레르노 대학교였다. 살레르노는 이탈리아의 한 도시이다. 이후에 한 대학이 프랑스에 생겼다. 파리 대학은 12세기에 설립되었다. 그 후로 얼마 지나지 않아 영국에서 옥스포드 대학이 문을 열었다.

초기 대학들은 종교에 초점을 두었다. 그들은 문법, 웅변, 논리학과 같은 과목들을 가르쳤다. 이것이 삼학이었다. 그들은 또한 수학, 기하학, 음악, 천문학을 가르쳤다. 이것이 사학이었다. 이러한 과목들을 배우며 대부분의 학생들은 성직자로서의 삶을 준비했다. 오랜 기간 동안 많은 학생들이 이러한 학교에 진학했다. 이 학교들 중 몇 곳은 오늘날에도 여전히 존재한다.

Reading Skills
Ⓓ

• **Exercise 6** • ——————————————— p.75

정답 Q1 Ⓓ   Q2 Ⓐ

해석   **토플과 토익 시험**

많은 학생들이 표준화된 시험들을 본다. 그들은 여러 가지 이유로 그 시험들을 치른다. 이러한 시험 중 어떤 것은 영어 능력을 테스트한다. 두 개의 주요한 영어 시험은 토플과 토익 시험이다.

외국 학생들이 종종 토플 시험을 본다. 그들은 미국에 있는 대학에 들어가기 위해서 이 시험을 치른다. 미국 학교에 들어가기 위해서는 높은 점수를 받아야 한다. 토플 시험은 읽기, 듣기, 말하기, 쓰기 능력을 측정한다. 많은 사람이 이 시험에 대비해 매우 열심히 공부한다.

다른 많은 학생들이 토익 시험을 본다. 이 시험은 거의 비즈니스를 위한 영어를 다룬다. 기업에 입사를 지원하는 사람들이 보통 이 시험을 본다. 그것은 듣기와 읽기 능력을 측정한다. 학생들은 영어 문법도 알아야 한다. 좋은 점수를 얻은 학생들은 우수한 기업에 입사할 수 있다.

Reading Skills
Ⓐ

• **Exercise 7** • ——————————————— p.76

정답 Q1 Ⓓ   Q2 Ⓑ

해석   **홈스쿨링**

오늘날 많은 미국의 아이들이 학교에 다니지 않는다. 대신 그들은 집에서 지낸다. 그들은 집에서 공부한다. 그들은 집에서 모든 수업을 듣는다. 그들의 부모 중 한 사람이 선생님 역할을 할 수도 있다. 홈스쿨링을 한 많은 학생들이 높은 성취도를 보인다. 그들은 종종 우수한 대학에도 입학한다.

학생들은 여러 가지 이유로 홈스쿨링을 한다. 때로는 부모가 그저 자신의 자녀를 직접 교육하고 싶은 경우도 있다. 그러나 많은 경우 아이들은 여러 다양한 과목들을 배우기 위해서 홈스쿨링을 한다. 공립 학교들은 대부분 영어, 역사, 수학, 과학을 가르친다. 또한 미술과 음악을 가르칠 수도 있다. 그러나 그러한 과목들이 전부이다. 반면에 홈스쿨링을 하는 학생들은 집에서 훨씬 더 많은 과목들을 배울 수 있다. 그들은 종교를 공부할 수 있다. 철학도 배울 수 있다. 또한 여러 다양한 언어들을 배울 수 있다.

Reading Skills
Ⓐ

• **Exercise 8** • ——————————————— p.77

정답 Q1 Ⓑ   Q2 Ⓓ

해석   **고등교육**

고등학교를 졸업한 후에 많은 학생들이 학업을 계속한다. 그들은 두 가지 다른 방법으로 공부를 할 수 있다. 먼저, 전통적인 고등교육이 있다. 그리고 다음으로는 대안 고등교육이 있다.

전통적으로, 많은 학생들이 공립이나 사립 대학에 들어간다. 그들은 또한 공립 전문대학에 입학할 수도 있다. 혹은 어떤 학생들은 사립 전문대학에 가기로 결정할 수도 있다. 사립 전문대학에 다니는 학생들은 2년 동안만 공부한다.

그러나 요즈음에는 대안 교육이 점점 더 대중화되고 있다. 그래서 어떤 학생들은 원격 교육을 받는다. 그들은 교실이 아니라 집에서 공부한다. 어떤 학생들은 사이버 대학에 간다. 그들은 모든 공부를 인터넷을 통해서 한다. 그리고 또 어떤 사람들은 사립 학원에 다닌다. 그러니까 이제 사람들은 학습에 대해 다양한 선택권을 가지고 있는 것이다.

Reading Skills
ⓒ

Grammar Point   p.78

✓ Grammar Check-Up

Ⓐ 1 an(the)   2 The   3 the   4 a   5 ¢

Ⓑ 1 a   2 ¢   3 an   4 the   5 ¢

ⓒ a, the, a, The, the, a, an, the

Vocabulary Review   p.80

Ⓐ 1 foreign
    2 brilliant
    3 junior
    4 handouts
    5 government

B 1 Ⓒ   2 Ⓒ   3 Ⓐ   4 Ⓓ   5 Ⓒ
C 1 Ⓒ   2 Ⓐ   3 Ⓓ   4 Ⓑ   5 Ⓐ
D 1 liberal
   2 blackboard
   3 focus
   4 homeschooling
   5 support

Practice Test — p.82

1 Ⓓ   2 Ⓒ   3 Ⓒ   4 Ⓓ   5 Ⓑ
6 Lecture: 1, 3, 5   Discussion: 2, 6

해석 강의 수업과 토론 수업

교사들은 매우 다양한 스타일을 가지고 있다. 하지만 대부분의 수업은 두 가지 유형으로 분류될 수 있다. 강의 수업과 토론 수업이 그것이다. 강의 수업에서는 주로 교사가 말을 한다. 토론 수업에서는 많은 학생들이 참여를 한다.

강의 수업이 좀 더 일반적이다. 이러한 수업에서는 대부분의 시간 동안 교사가 말을 한다. 학생들은 강의를 듣고 필기를 한다. 이러한 수업으로 학생들은 많은 것을 배울 수 있다. 이러한 방법은 역사, 수학, 과학과 같은 주제에 이상적이다. 많은 경우, 교사들은 학생들의 질문을 허용한다. 하지만 학생들의 참여를 독려하지는 않는다. 대신 학생들에게 최대한 많은 정보를 전달하는 것에 초점을 맞춘다.

토론 수업에는 종종 강의가 포함된다. 하지만 교사들은 학생들의 참여 또한 독려한다. 그들은 학생들이 질문을 하도록 유도한다. 또한 학생들이 자신만의 의견을 제시하도록 권장한다. 많은 경우, 교사들은 그룹 토론을 구성한다. 이렇게 하면 학생들이 서로 이야기를 나눌 수 있게 된다. 영어와 사회과 수업이 이러한 유형을 따를 수 있다.

두 가지 방식 모두 효과적이다. 그리고 학생들은 이런 방식들을 통해 학습할 수 있다. 하지만 대부분의 학생들은 둘 중 하나를 선호한다.

CHAPTER 5 Economics

Understanding TOEFL Question Types & Reading Skills — p.86

① Question Types ▸ Sample Question
Ⓑ

해석 물물교환

요즘에 사람들은 돈을 사용한다. 그러나 예전에는 돈이 없었다. 그래서 사람들은 물물교환을 했다. 이것은 하나의 물건을 다른 물건과 바꾸는 것을 의미한다. 사람들은 자신이 가진 물건의 가치를 결정했다. 아마도 어떤 농부는 토마토 열 개를 구두 두 켤레와 바꾸었을 것이다. 혹은 어떤 어부는 물고기 한 마리를 사과 세 개와 교환했을 것이다.

② Reading Skills ▸ Check-Up
Ⓓ

• Exercise 1 • — p.88

정답 Ⓑ

해석 세금

모든 정부는 돈이 필요하다. 돈이 없으면 정부는 다양한 서비스를 제공할 수 없다. 그래서 정부는 돈을 거둬야 한다. 돈을 거두는 한 가지 방법은 세금을 통해서이다. 가장 일반적인 세금은 소득세와 판매세이다. 그렇지만, 다른 세금들도 많이 있다. 사람들은 집에 대한 재산세를 내야 한다. 다른 나라에서 수입하는 물건에 대한 관세도 있다.

Reading Skills
Ⓓ

• Exercise 2 • — p.89

정답 Ⓐ

해석 애덤 스미스

애덤 스미스는 1723년에 태어나서 1790년까지 살았다. 그는 세계에서 가장 중요한 경제학자 중 한 사람이었다. 그는 국부론이라는 책을 썼다. 책에서 그는 자유 시장 경제 이론을 제시했다. 그 이론에서 정부는 시장에 개입하지 않는다. 대신에, 사람들은 그들이 원하는 것은 무엇이든지 할 수 있다. 사람들은 또한 가능한 한 많은 돈을 벌기 위해 노력한다.

Reading Skills
Ⓑ

• Exercise 3 • — p.90

정답 Ⓓ

해석 돈

많은 다양한 종류의 돈이 있다. 먼저, 사람들은 주로 동전과 지폐를 사용한다. 사람들은 이것을 현금으로 쓴다. 그에 더해 사람들은 다른 종류의 화폐를 사용할 수 있다. 예를 들어, 어떤 사람들은 수표로 계산을 한다. 수표를 사용하면, 은행은 어떤 사람의 은행계좌에서 돈을 인출할 것이다. 또 어떤 사람들은 신용카드를 돈으로 사용하는 것을 선호한다.

Reading Skills
Ⓐ

• Exercise 4 • — p.91

정답 Ⓒ

해석 대출

돈이 필요한 경우, 사람들은 은행에서 대출을 받을 수 있다. 대출은 개인에게 여러 목적으로 사용될 돈을 제공한다. 여기에는 주택이나 차량 구입, 혹은 사업 운영 자금이 포함된다. 대출자가 지켜야 하는 대출 조건들이 있다. 대출금은 할부로 상환된다. 그것은 주로 달마다 이루어진다. 또한 대출 이자를 납부해야 한다.

Reading Skills
Ⓓ

• Exercise 5 • —————————————————— p.92

정답 Q1 ⓒ   Q2 ⓓ

해석   불경기와 불황

대부분의 국가들의 경제는 시간이 지남에 따라 나아진다. 이것은 보통 매우 천천히 진행된다. 그렇더라도 경제는 거의 항상 더 좋아지는 편이다. 그러나 때로는 어떤 국가의 경제가 나빠질 수도 있다. 사람들은 일자리를 잃을 수도 있다. 그들은 돈을 더 적게 벌기 시작한다. 기업들 또한 손실을 입고 파산한다. 이러한 상황은 심지어 수개월 동안 일어날 수도 있다. 부정적인 성장이 6개월 이상 지속되면, 사람들은 이 시기를 불경기라고 부른다.

불경기는 아주 오랜 기간 동안 지속될 수 있다. 때로는 더 악화될 수도 있다. 사람들은 이 시기를 불황이라고 부른다. 불황은 불경기가 심각한 것을 말한다.

1929년에 미국에서 대공황이 시작되었다. 그것은 2차 세계 대전이 일어날 때까지 10년 이상 계속되었다. 그것은 미국 경제에 심각한 악영향을 끼쳤다.

Reading Skills

ⓑ

• Exercise 6 • —————————————————— p.93

정답 Q1 ⓐ   Q2 ⓐ

해석   경제 체제

경제 체제에는 여러 종류가 있다. 대부분의 국가들은 자본주의 경제 체제를 따른다. 이것은 사유재산제에 바탕을 둔 체제이다. 거의 모든 경우에 사람들은 기업을 소유하고 이윤을 위해 기업을 경영한다. 그들은 가능한 한 많은 돈을 벌고 싶어 한다. 자본주의 경제 체제에서 정부는 경제에 개입하지 않으려고 노력한다. 그 체제는 일반적으로 개별 시민의 경제활동을 방해하지 않는다. 그것은 시민 스스로 경제를 운용하도록 한다. 그러나 때로는 기업과 관련된 법이 통과되기도 한다.

사회주의 경제 체제는 이와 다르다. 사회주의 경제 체제 아래에서 정부는 대부분의 기업을 소유한다. 이윤 창출에 대한 비중이 적다. 대신에, 사람들은 공동체의 복지에 대해 더 많이 생각한다. 사회주의 경제 체제에서는 정부가 보통 다양한 산업을 국유화한다. 이것은 정부가 산업을 인수해서 그것을 운용한다는 것을 의미한다.

Reading Skills

ⓑ

• Exercise 7 • —————————————————— p.94

정답 Q1 ⓒ   Q2 ⓑ

해석   주식

많은 기업들이 개인의 소유이다. 그래서 오로지 한 사람 혹은 하나의 동업 집단이 기업을 소유한다. 그러나 유한회사라고 불리는 기업들이 있다. 많은 사람들이 하나의 유한회사를 소유할 수 있다. 유한회사들은 주식을 발행한다. 주식은 회사의 지분이다. 유한회사들은 일반적으로 수백만 개의 지분을 발행한다. 이런 방식으로 수천 명의 다른 사람들이 한 회사의 공동 소유주가 될 수 있다.

사람들은 주식의 지분을 사고 팔 수 있다. 보통 이것을 주식시장에서 한다. 가장 유명한 주식시장은 미국에 있는 뉴욕 증권거래소이다. 사람들은 매일 수백만 주의 주식을 거래한다. 주식 가격은 쉴 새 없이 오르내린다. 사람들은 언제나 저가에 사서 고가에 팔려고 노력한다.

Reading Skills

ⓒ

• Exercise 8 • —————————————————— p.95

정답 Q1 ⓓ   Q2 ⓑ

해석   공급과 수요

기업들은 항상 제품을 만든다. 그러나 그들은 여러 제품을 다양한 수량으로 만든다. 구할 수 있는 제품의 양을 공급이라고 한다. 이것은 항상 정확히 수치화된다. 사람들은 보통 특정한 상품을 사고 싶어 한다. 물론 어떤 제품들은 다른 제품보다 훨씬 더 인기 있다. 사람들이 특정한 제품을 원하는 비율을 수요라고 한다. 이것은 계산하기가 더 어렵다. 그래서 경제학자들은 항상 수요를 측정하기 위해 노력한다.

공급과 수요 둘 다 항상 가격에 영향을 미친다. 어떤 경우에는 수요가 적은 반면 공급이 많다. 그러면 가격 또한 내려간다. 그러나 수요는 많고 공급이 적을 수도 있다. 그러면 가격은 올라간다. 매장들은 항상 제품의 가격을 결정하기 위해서 공급과 수요를 이용한다.

Reading Skills

ⓒ

Grammar Point   p.96

Grammar Check-Up

A 1 Consequently
   2 Otherwise
   3 For example
   4 yet
   5 then

B 1 ⓒ   2 ⓐ   3 ⓓ   4 ⓐ   5 ⓑ

C Therefore, In other words, Nevertheless, Then, In addition, So, Likewise

Vocabulary Review   p.98

A 1 economics
   2 rate
   3 market
   4 Depression
   5 bankrupt

B 1 ⓑ   2 ⓐ   3 ⓓ   4 ⓑ   5 ⓒ

C 1 ⓑ   2 ⓓ   3 ⓒ   4 ⓐ   5 ⓒ

D 1 checking
   2 available
   3 private
   4 supply
   5 economist

Practice Test   p.100

1 ⓒ   2 ⓑ   3 ⓓ   4 ⓐ   5 ⓐ   6 ②, ⑤, ⑥

해석 역사상 존재해 온 다양한 유형의 화폐

오늘날에는 많은 유형의 화폐가 존재한다. 예를 들어 사람들은 현금, 신용카드, 혹은 수표로 상품과 서비스에 대한 비용을 지불할 수 있다. 심지어 비트코인과 같은 가상화폐를 사용할 수도 있다. 하지만 사람들이 사용해 온 화폐의 유형이 이러한 것만 있는 것은 아니다. 역사를 통틀어 다른 유형의 화폐들이 존재해 왔다.

기원전 1,200년경 어떤 사람들은 조개 껍질을 화폐로 사용했다. 로마인들은 주로 소금으로 병사의 급여를 지급했다. 또한 과거에 사람들은 소, 가죽, 돌, 그리고 담배를 화폐로 사용하기도 했다. 금속은 기원전 2,000년경에 화폐로서 처음 사용되었다. 바빌론에서 이런 일이 있었다. 하지만 최초의 주화는 리디아에서 등장했다. 기원전 7세기에 있었던 일이다. 이 주화는 합금으로 만들어졌다.

동전의 사용은 빠르게 확산되었다. 사람들은 구리, 은, 금, 그리고 기타 금속들로 동전을 만들었다. 이후 중국인들이 종이로 지폐를 만들었다. 서기 1,000년경에 일어난 일이었다. 시간이 지나면서 동전과 지폐는 어디에서나 일반적인 것이 되었다. 다른 종류의 화폐들도 존재하지만, 사람들은 오늘날에도 여전히 이들을 사용하고 있다.

CHAPTER 6 Sociology

Understanding TOEFL Question Types & Reading Skills   p.104

1 Question Types ▸ Sample Question
ⓐ

해석 자원봉사

많은 사람들이 종종 자선활동에 참여한다. 그들은 어딘가에서 자원하여 일한다. 그들은 병원이나 도서관, 혹은 노숙인 쉼터로 갈 수도 있다. 그들은 그러한 장소에 가서 보통 몇 시간 동안 활동을 한다. 그리고 그들은 심지어 돈을 전혀 받지 않는다.

2 Reading Skills ▸ Check-Up
ⓑ

• Exercise 1 •   p.106

정답 ⓓ

해석 이혼

결혼한 부부에게는 때때로 많은 문제들이 생긴다. 그들은 보통 돈과 재산 문제 때문에 싸운다. 때로는 자녀들 때문에 말다툼을 하기도 한다. 그들은 자신들의 문제를 해결하려고 노력할지도 모른다. 하지만 보통 그렇게 하지 못한다. 이런 경우, 그들은 이혼을 하게 된다. 이혼은 한 부부의 결혼생활을 법적으로 끝내는 것이다. 어쨌거나 이것은 여러 가지 문제를 일으킬 수 있다. 특히 이것은 자녀들에게 오랫동안 나쁜 영향을 미칠 수 있다.

Reading Skills
ⓐ

• Exercise 2 •   p.107

정답 ⓒ

해석 스포츠 단체

미국의 많은 성인들과 아이들이 스포츠 리그에 참가한다. 시와 자치주가 리그들을 운영한다. 그들은 보통 축구, 야구, 농구, 미식축구 리그를 운영한다. 이 리그들을 통해 사람들은 운동을 하고 팀 스포츠를 즐기게 된다. 그리고 아이들이 팀워크를 배우고 좋은 친구를 사귀는 데 도움이 된다. 이러한 리그들은 대부분 비용이 많이 들지 않는다. 팀들은 주로 주말이나 저녁에 경기를 한다.

Reading Skills
ⓓ

• Exercise 3 •   p.108

정답 ⓒ

해석 대중교통

많은 도시의 사람들이 자가용을 소유하고 있지 않다. 개인용 차량은 너무 비싸다. 또한 도시에는 개인용 차량을 위한 공간이 충분하지 않다. 그래서 대부분의 도시에는 대중교통 시스템이 갖추어져 있다. 이것은 버스, 지하철, 통근 기차와 같은 시스템들이다. 그 시스템들은 시민들에게 저렴하고 효율적인 교통 수단을 제공한다. 또한 교통 체증을 줄이는 데에도 도움을 준다.

Reading Skills
ⓑ

• Exercise 4 •   p.109

정답 ⓐ

해석 소셜 미디어

소셜 미디어는 젊은이들에게 많은 즐거움을 준다. 하지만 소셜 미디어에는 단점도 많이 있다. 어떤 젊은이들은 소셜 미디어에 중독되어 있다. 그들은 소셜 미디어를 이용하느라 매일 몇 시간씩을 소비한다. 그 결과 학업을 소홀히 하게 된다. 그들은 운동을 충분히 하지 않고, 스포츠 활동 또한 하지 않는다. 어떤 이들은 다른 또래들과 소통하는 데 어려움을 겪기도 한다.

Reading Skills
ⓓ

12

• Exercise 5 • p.110

정답 Q1 Ⓒ Q2 Ⓐ

해석 교외 지역

오랫동안 사람들은 시골이나 도시 둘 중 한 곳에 살았다. 그러나 시골은 모든 것에서 매우 멀었다. 도시 또한 보통은 너무 복잡했다. 그러다가 1900년대에 사람들은 자동차를 사기 시작했다. 그러자 더 빨리 그리고 더 멀리 이동할 수 있게 되었다. 그 결과 사람들은 도시를 떠나기 시작했다. 그러나 그들은 시골로 이주하지 않았다. 대신에 그들은 교외 지역으로 이사를 갔다.

교외 지역은 도시 근교의 시내와 같은 곳이다. 그곳에는 대부분 주거단지가 있다. 그곳에는 대체로 공장이나 회사가 거의 없다. 교외 지역에는 쇼핑몰이나 슈퍼마켓이 있을 수 있다. 교외 지역은 도시보다 훨씬 더 살기 좋은 장소이다. 사람들은 대부분 도시에서 일을 한다. 그러나 그들은 교외 지역에서 산다. 자동차 덕택에 그들은 이러한 삶을 살 수 있게 되었다.

Reading Skills

Ⓐ

• Exercise 6 • p.111

정답 Q1 Ⓓ Q2 Ⓐ

해석 외부인 출입 제한 주택단지

전 세계 어떤 지역들은 점점 위험해지고 있다. 그래서 많은 사람들이 외부인 출입 제한 주택단지에 사는 것을 선택하고 있다. 이곳은 작은 도시와 같다. 큰 울타리가 전체 단지를 둘러 싸고 있다. 사람들이 그곳으로 출입하기 위해서는 정문을 통과해야만 한다. 많은 경우에 경비원들이 이러한 단지들을 지키고 있다.

이러한 단지들 안에는 많은 것들이 있다. 사람들이 사는 주택이 그곳에 있다. 보통 쇼핑센터와 슈퍼마켓 또한 있다. 어떤 경우에는 그 안에 학교도 있다. 이러한 곳에서 많은 경우, 사람들은 거주 구역 밖으로 그렇게 자주 나갈 필요가 없다. 미국에서는 이런 단지들이 점점 인기를 얻고 있다. 그러나 요즈음에는 중국과 남아프리카 공화국 등 다른 나라들에서도 이런 곳들을 짓고 있다.

Reading Skills

Ⓒ

• Exercise 7 • p.112

정답 Q1 Ⓓ Q2 Ⓓ

해석 한 부모 가정

지난 수십 년간 점점 더 많은 미국인들이 이혼을 하고 있다. 안타깝게도 이러한 부부들에게는 보통 자녀가 있다. 그래서 그들은 집에서 한 부모와만 함께 살면서 성장해야 한다. 사회학자들은 이러한 가정을 한 부모 가정이라고 부른다.

한 부모 가정에서 자란 아이들은 종종 어려운 시기를 겪는다. 그들은 보통 어머니나 아버지를 그리워한다. 그들은 학교에서 다른 학생들만큼 학업을 성취하지 못할 수도 있다. 그리고 때때로 그들은 정서 문제를 겪는다. 이러한 것들은 나중에 인생에서 큰 문제들을 일으킬 수 있다. 대부분의 연구자들은 아이들이 양부모님과 함께 자라는 것이 더 낫다고 생각한다. 그러나 이것이 많은 아이들에게 가능한 일은 아니다. 그래서 그들과 함께 사는 한 부모는 그 아이들이 잘 자라나도록 정말 많은 노력을 기울여야 한다.

Reading Skills

Ⓐ

• Exercise 8 • p.113

정답 Q1 Ⓒ Q2 Ⓐ

해석 또래 압력

십대들은 종종 힘든 시기를 겪는다. 가장 어려운 것들 중 하나는 또래 집단으로부터 받는 사회적 압력이다. 그들의 또래는 다른 십대들이다. 어떤 십대들은 맥주를 마시거나 담배를 피우는 것 같은 행동을 한다. 많은 십대들은 이러한 것들을 하기를 원치 않는다. 그러나 불량한 십대들은 그들이 그렇게 하도록 만든다. 많은 십대들이 자신이 이러한 것들을 하지 않으면 소외될 것이라고 믿는다. 그래서 그들은 자진해서 이러한 나쁜 행동들을 한다.

이것은 많은 문제를 일으킬 수 있다. 예를 들어 어떤 십대들은 파티에 가서 맥주를 마신다. 그들은 실제로는 술을 마시고 싶지 않다. 그러나 어떤 경우 그들은 취하게 된다. 그러고나서 그들은 차를 운전한다. 그 결과 사고를 낼 수도 있다. 어떤 경우에는 다치거나 심지어 죽기도 한다. 이것은 또래 집단으로부터 받는 사회적 압력이 얼마나 심각한 해악이 될 수 있는지를 보여준다.

Reading Skills

Ⓒ

Grammar Point p.114

Grammar Check-Up

A 1 ⓑ 2 ⓒ 3 ⓑ 4 ⓑ 5 ⓓ

B 1 ⓒ 2 ⓑ 3 ⓑ

C 1 for 2 with 3 of 4 from 5 from

Vocabulary Review p.116

A 1 Peer
   2 interact
   3 shelters
   4 vehicle
   5 fence

B 1 Ⓓ 2 Ⓐ 3 Ⓒ 4 Ⓒ 5 Ⓓ

C 1 Ⓐ 2 Ⓑ 3 Ⓓ 4 Ⓐ 5 Ⓓ

D 1 decades
   2 drawbacks
   3 emotional
   4 surrounds
   5 purchase

Practice Test　　　　　　　　　　　　p.118

1 Ⓐ　　2 Ⓒ　　3 Ⓐ　　4 Ⓐ　　5 Ⓓ　　6 [1], [4], [6]

해석　　　　　여성의 역할 변화

역사의 대부분의 기간 동안, 남성과 여성의 역할은 분리되어 있었다. 전통적으로 남성들이 부양자였다. 그들은 가족들이 먹을 음식을 조달하기 위해, 사냥을 하거나 농사를 지었다. 또는 가족을 위해 일을 해 돈을 벌었다. 반면에 여성은 주로 집에 있었다. 그들은 자녀를 돌보고 양육했다. 수천 년 동안 이렇게 살아왔다. 그러나 최근에 여성의 역할이 변화하고 있다.

첫째로, 요즘에는 많은 여성들이 집에서 나와 일을 하고 있다. 과거에는 일부 여성들만이 일을 하였다. 그렇지만 그들은 대체로 교사나 간호사, 혹은 비서로서 주로 일을 하였다. 그러던 중 19세기와 20세기에 페미니즘이 시작되었다. 이 이론은 남성과 여성이 평등하다고 주장한다. 페미니즘 덕분에 많은 여성들이 다양한 종류의 직업을 갖기 시작했다. 오늘날, 기술자나 의사, 변호사, 조종사로서 일하는 등 많은 다양한 직업에 종사하는 여성들이 있다.

두 번째로, 요즘에는 많은 여성들이 자녀를 직접 양육하지 않는다. 수많은 일하는 여성들이 자녀를 보육 시설에 보낸다. 그곳에서 아이들은 같은 연령대의 다른 아이들과 놀 수 있다. 시설이 자녀를 돌보는 것이다. 그렇게 함으로써, 여성들은 일을 할 수 있다. 아버지들 또한 때때로 전업으로 아이들을 돌본다. 이러한 경우에는 여성들이 대신 일을 하고 돈을 번다. 이것은 여성의 전통적인 역할과는 매우 다르다.

CHAPTER 7　Exploration

Understanding TOEFL Question Types & Reading Skills　　　p.122

❶ Question Types ▸ Sample Question

Ⓐ

해석　　　　　우주 탐험

사람들은 우주를 탐험하길 오랫동안 간절히 원해 왔다. 1957년에 최초의 인공위성이 궤도에 올랐다. 거기에서 더 나아가 유인 우주선이 우주로 갔다. 그리고 또 다른 인류는 달을 탐험했다. 미래에 인류는 반드시 화성과 다른 행성들을 탐험할 것이다.

❷ Reading Skills ▸ Check-Up

In addition

• Exercise 1 •　　　　　　　　　　　　p.124

해석　　　　　크리스토퍼 콜럼버스

크리스토퍼 콜럼버스는 이탈리아 출신의 탐험가였다. 1492년에 그는 드넓은 대서양을 횡단했다. 그에게는 세 척의 배가 있었다. *핀타*, *니나*, *산타 마리아*라는 배였다. 8주가 지나서야 그는 아메리카에 도착했다. 후에, 콜럼버스는 신세계로 세 번의 항해를 더 했다. 콜럼버스 덕분에 다른 많은 사람들도 아메리카 대륙으로 항해했다.

Reading Skills

Ⓑ

• Exercise 2 •　　　　　　　　　　　　p.125

정답 [1]

해석　　　　　존 캐벗

1497년 존 캐벗은 영국을 떠났다. 그는 대서양을 가로질러 서쪽으로 항해했다. 그는 아시아에 도착하기를 바라고 있었다. 대신에, 그는 캐나다를 발견했다. 그리고 그는 수 세기 전 바이킹족 이후에 그곳에 간 최초의 유럽인이 되었다. (그의 여행은 매우 성공적으로 여겨졌다.) 다음 해에 캐벗은 대서양을 가로질러 다시 돌아왔다. 그의 다섯 척의 배 중 한 척은 아일랜드에 도착했다. 하지만 다른 네 척의 배는 사라졌다. 캐벗과 그의 선원들에게 어떤 일이 있었는지는 아무도 모른다.

Reading Skills

1 And　　2 But

• Exercise 3 •　　　　　　　　　　　　p.126

정답 Ⓒ

해석　　　　　폰세 데 레온

폰세 데 레온은 16세기의 스페인 출신 탐험가였다. 그는 대부분의 신세계 탐험가들과는 달랐다. 그는 금도 명예도 원하지 않았다. 대신에 그는 젊음의 샘을 찾아 다녔다. 사람들 그것을 '생명수'라고도 불렀다. 그는 그것이 사람들을 젊어지게 한다고 믿었다. 여정 중에 그는 플로리다를 발견했다. 그는 그 샘이 그곳에 있다고 생각했다. 그러나 그는 결코 그것을 찾지 못했다.

Reading Skills

Ⓓ

• Exercise 4 •　　　　　　　　　　　　p.127

정답 [4]

해석　　　　　제임스 쿡

제임스 쿡은 영국의 중요한 탐험가였다. 그는 10년 이상을 태평양을 항해하면서 보냈다. 그리고 그는 오스트레일리아의 해안 지도를 만들었다. 이것은 그 대륙의 지도를 그리는 데 도움을 주었다. 그는 그 지역의 많은 군도를 발견하기도 했다. 더구나 그는 하와이에 정박한 최초의 유럽인이었다. 그는 그 섬을 샌드위치 아일랜드라고 이름 지었다. (불행하게도 그는 그곳을 여행하던 중 몇몇 원주민들과 싸움이 붙어 죽었다.)

Reading Skills

1 And　　2 Furthermore

• Exercise 5 •　　　　　　　　　　　　p.128

정답 Q1 Ⓐ　　Q2 [1]

해석 　　　　　　　　　　바이킹

바이킹은 북유럽 사람들이다. 그들은 맹렬한 전사이자, 투사였다. 그리고 그들은 대양을 항해하는 것을 사랑했다. 그들은 또한 위대한 탐험가였다. 8세기부터 11세기까지 그들은 대서양 곳곳을 항해했다. 그들은 영국을 방문했다. 그들은 심지어 콘스탄티노플과 러시아에도 갔다.

그들은 또한 대서양을 횡단했다. 986년에 그들은 그린란드에 정박했다. 에이리크 힌 라우디와 그의 아들인 레이프 에이릭손이 그곳에 갔다. (이 두 사람은 소수 정예의 바이킹들을 함께 데려갔다.) 그러나 그들은 서쪽으로 항해를 계속했다. 그들은 마침내 북아메리카에 도착했다. 그들은 북아메리카에 간 최초의 유럽인들이었다. 그러나 바이킹들은 그곳에 머무르지 않았다. 대신에, 그들은 유럽으로 되돌아왔다. 그래서 오랫동안 아무도 아메리카에 대해서 알지 못했다.

Reading Skills

Ⓓ

• **Exercise 6** • ───────── p.129

정답 Q1 Ⓓ Q2 ■

해석 　　　　　　　　　마르코 폴로

13세기에 대부분의 유럽 사람들은 아시아에 대해서 아무것도 알지 못했다. 그러나 그들은 아시아에 대해서 몹시 궁금해했다. 그래서 몇몇 유럽인들이 동쪽으로 여행을 떠났다. 그러나 그들 중 많은 이들이 돌아오지 못했다. 마르코 폴로는 이탈리아인 모험가였다. 그는 실크로드를 따라 아시아를 향해 동쪽으로 여행했다. 수년 동안 아무도 그를 보지 못했다. 그래서 사람들은 그가 죽었다고 믿었다. 그러나 24년이 지난 후, 갑자기 마르코 폴로가 유럽으로 돌아왔다.

그는 중국을 향해 계속해서 여행을 했었다. (그곳으로 가는 길에 그는 많은 모험을 겪었다.) 그는 몽골의 쿠빌라이 칸을 만났다. 그는 실제로 칸의 고문이 되었다. 그는 아시아에서 아주 부유해졌다. 그러나 그는 여전히 집으로 되돌아가고 싶어 했다. 그가 돌아온 후에, 많은 사람들이 그의 여행에 대해 들었다. 그래서 점점 더 많은 유럽인들이 아시아를 방문하기 시작했다.

Reading Skills

1 So 2 After

• **Exercise 7** • ───────── p.130

정답 Q1 ■ Q2 Ⓒ

해석 　　　　　　　　　해저 탐험

인류는 지구 표면의 대부분을 탐험해 왔다. (실제로 사람들은 이제 지구의 표면에 대해 많은 것을 안다.) 그러나 여전히 대부분의 인류가 탐험하지 못한 한 곳이 있다. 바로 바닷속 영역이다. 바다는 여전히 신비스러운 장소로 남아 있다. 그러나 이제 더 많은 사람들이 그것의 비밀에 대해 알아가고 있다. 그들은 몇 가지 방법들을 통해 이렇게 한다.

어떤 사람은 스쿠버 다이빙 장비를 이용한다. 그들은 수영을 하는 동안 장비를 착용한다. 이렇게 함으로써 그들은 물속에서 숨을 쉴 수 있다. 또 다른 사람들은 잠수함을 타고 바다를 탐험한다. 잠수함은 바닷속을 여행할 수 있다. 어떤 사람들은 바닷속에서 수개월 동안 지낼 수 있다. 잠수함 덕분에 사람들은 바다에 대해서 매우 많은 것을 알아가고 있다. 또한 다른 종류의 잠수정들도 있다. 이런 잠수정들은 바닷속 깊이 잠수할 수 있다. 그것들은 많은 새로운 종의 물고기들을 발견하고 있다.

Reading Skills

Ⓒ

• **Exercise 8** • ───────── p.131

정답 Q1 ④ Q2 Ⓑ

해석 　　　　　　　　　　지도

지도가 없다면 사람들은 쉽게 길을 잃을 수 있다. 그래서 지도는 탐험가들에게 정말 중요하다. 그들의 지도는 매우 정확해야 한다. 안타깝게도 오래 전에는 많은 지도들이 부정확한 정보를 담고 있었다. 혹은 지도가 대상들 사이의 거리를 틀리게 보여주기도 했다. (이러한 문제들은 종종 사람들을 매우 헷갈리게 했다.)

가장 흔한 종류의 지도는 지리적 지도이다. 이 지도들은 땅의 특정 영역을 보여준다. 이 영역은 매우 클 수도 있고 작을 수도 있다. 영역이 작을수록 지도는 더 상세한 정보를 담고 있다. 지도에서 비례는 매우 중요하다. 이것은 대상이 서로 얼마나 가까이 있는지를 보여준다.

지도 덕분에 지구에 대한 인류의 지식은 크게 발전하였다. 사람들이 더 많이 탐험하기 시작할수록 지도는 점점 더 정확해졌다. 오늘날 사람들이 사용하는 지도는 전반적으로 품질이 우수하다.

Reading Skills

1 Or 2 As

Grammar Point　　　　　　　　p.132

Grammar Check-Up

Ⓐ 1 by
　2 on
　3 in
　4 to
　5 until

Ⓑ 1 on
　2 over
　3 after
　4 by
　5 front

Ⓒ by, in, until, on, before, for, on

Vocabulary Review　　　　　　p.134

Ⓐ 1 species
　2 extremely
　3 vast
　4 equipment
　5 traveled

Ⓑ 1 Ⓐ 2 Ⓓ 3 Ⓓ 4 Ⓑ 5 Ⓒ

C 1 Ⓑ 2 Ⓓ 3 Ⓒ 4 Ⓐ 5 Ⓐ

D 1 submersible
   2 secrets
   3 discover
   4 planets
   5 mysterious

Practice Test   p.136

1 Ⓑ 2 Ⓒ 3 Ⓑ 4 Ⓓ 5 ④ 6 ②, ③, ⑥

해석   루이스 클라크 탐험대

18세기 말까지만 해도 미국은 작은 국가였다. 대부분 미시시피강 동부 지역에 한정된 땅이었다. 그러나 이것은 1803년에 바뀌었다. 그해에 토머스 제퍼슨 대통령이 나폴레옹에게서 프랑스령인 루이지애나 땅을 매입했다. 이곳은 거대한 땅이었다. 그곳은 현재 미국의 중부 지역에 해당했다. 제퍼슨은 그 새로운 영토를 탐험하고 싶었다. (그 이전에는 아주 소수의 사람들만이 이 미지의 땅에 가 본 적이 있었다.) 그래서 그는 루이스 클라크 탐험대를 보냈다.

메리웨더 루이스와 윌리엄 클라크는 그 탐험대의 두 대장이었다. 그들은 1804년에 출발했다. 그들은 1806년이 되어서야 돌아왔다. 그 탐험대는 몇 가지 목표를 가지고 있었다. 그들은 루이지애나 영토를 탐험하고, 그곳의 식물과 동물들에 대해 조사해야 했다. 그들은 그곳의 원주민 부족들에 대해서 연구해야 했다. 그들은 또한 태평양으로 가는 길을 발견하기 위해 애써야 했다. 그들은 모든 목표를 성취했다.

그러나 그 여행은 쉽지 않았다. 그들은 여정 동안 많은 어려움에 직면했다. 그들은 때로 배로 여행했다. 하지만 보통 육로를 따라 걸어야 했다. 그들은 많은 원주민 부족들을 만났다. 다행히 그들 대부분이 호의적이었다. 그들이 미개척지에서 보낸 두 해의 겨울은 매우 혹독했다. 그럼에도, 그들은 태평양에 도달할 수 있었고 그러고나서 동부로 돌아왔다. 이것은 다른 많은 사람들이 더 많은 탐험을 할 수 있는 문을 열어 주었다.

CHAPTER 8 Environment

Understanding TOEFL Question Types & Reading Skills   p.140

1 Question Types ▶ Sample Question

Q1 Ⓑ, Ⓒ
Q2 Liquid Fuels: Ⓐ, Ⓓ   Solid Fuels: Ⓑ, Ⓒ

해석   연료

연료는 중요한 에너지 자원이다. 액체 연료가 한 예이다. 이것은 죽은 식물이나 동물들로 만들어진다. 가장 흔한 액체 연료는 가솔린이다. 다른 종류로는 디젤연료가 있다. 차량은 이러한 종류의 연료를 사용한다. 그 외에 고체 연료가 있다. 사람들은 에너지 생산이나 건물 난방에 이 연료를 사용한다. 나무와 석탄이 이러한 연료의 두 가지 형태이다.

2 Reading Skills ▶ Check-Up

plants, coal

• Exercise 1   p.142

정답 Ⓐ, Ⓒ

해석   열대 우림

열대 우림은 지구상에서 가장 독특한 지역에 속한다. 열대 우림은 정말 변화무쌍한 장소이다. 많은 종의 동물들이 그곳에서 서식하고 있다. 포유류, 조류, 그리고 파충류 등 모든 종이 이 숲 지대에 산다.

아마존과 같은 열대 우림에는 셀 수 없을 정도로 많은 종의 나무와 식물들이 있다. 그것들은 지구의 산소 공급량의 대부분을 생산하는 역할을 한다. 열대 우림이 없다면, 지구는 지금과는 매우 다른 모습일 것이다.

Reading Skills

Reptiles, oxygen

• Exercise 2   p.143

정답 Ⓐ, Ⓓ

해석   재활용

사람들은 너무 많은 천연자원을 사용한다. 지구의 자원은 고갈되고 있다. 그래서 재활용이 매우 중요하다. 그렇게 함으로써, 기업들은 지구의 자원을 계속해서 재사용할 수 있다.

사람들은 많은 것을 재활용할 수 있다. 그들은 병으로 유리를, 신문과 잡지로 종이를 재활용할 수 있다. 그들은 또한 캔으로 금속을 재활용할 수 있다. 재활용을 함으로써, 사람들은 지구의 자원을 절약하는 데 도움을 줄 수 있다.

Reading Skills

bottles, cans, recycling

• Exercise 3   p.144

정답 Ⓑ, Ⓓ

해석   산성비

때때로 오염물질이 대기 중으로 올라간다. 구름이 보통 그것을 흡수한다. 나중에 이러한 구름에서 비가 내린다. 그러나 이러한 비는 더럽고 유해하다. 사람들은 그것을 산성비라고 부른다.

산성비는 많은 동물들을 죽인다. 산성비 때문에 어떤 호수에는 생물이 살지 않는다. 오늘날 사람들은 산성비를 방지하려고 애쓰고 있다. 그러나 그것은 여전히 많은 지역에서 문제가 되고 있다.

Reading Skills

Clouds, clouds, lakes

• Exercise 4   p.145

정답 Ⓑ, Ⓓ

해석 **침식**

침식은 땅이 점점 깎일 때 이루어진다. 물, 바람, 그리고 얼음이 종종 침식을 일으킬 수 있다. 이들로 인해 땅의 형태가 바뀔 수 있다. 침식은 천천히 이루어질 수 있다. 예를 들어 수천 년에 걸쳐 이루어질 수도 있다. 혹은 빠르게 이루어질 수도 있다. 허리케인으로 인해 몇 시간 내에 땅이 침식될 수도 있다. 침식 때문에 땅의 모습은 항상 바뀌고 있다.

Reading Skills

water, face

• **Exercise 5** • ──────────────── p.146

정답 At Home: Ⓐ, Ⓕ   Outside the Home: Ⓒ, Ⓓ

해석 **쓰레기 줄이기**

쓰레기는 요즘 아주 큰 문제이다. 그래서 사람들은 쓰레기를 너무 많이 만들어내지 않기 위한 방법들을 생각해야 한다. 사람들은 쓰레기를 두 곳에서 줄일 수 있다. 가정에서나 집 밖에서 이렇게 할 수 있다.

첫째로, 사람들은 가정에서 너무 많은 쓰레기를 만들지 말아야 한다. 유리, 종이, 플라스틱, 금속을 재활용하려고 노력할 수 있다. 종이 냅킨 대신에 천 냅킨을 재사용할 수 있다. 또한 재충전이 가능한 배터리를 구매할 수도 있다. 그렇게 하면 사람들은 배터리를 버리지 않아도 될 것이다.

집 밖에서도 많은 일을 할 수 있다. 식료품점에서 새로운 가방을 받는 대신에 자신의 가방을 가지고 갈 수 있다. 또한 중고품을 살 수도 있다.

Reading Skills

cloth napkins, batteries, bags, used items

• **Exercise 6** • ──────────────── p.147

정답 Hurricanes: Ⓒ, Ⓔ   Typhoons: Ⓑ, Ⓓ

해석 **허리케인과 태풍**

자연은 매우 난폭할 수 있다. 거대한 폭풍우는 대개 갑자기 형성된다. 허리케인과 태풍이라는 두 종류의 폭풍우가 있다. 그 둘은 실제로는 같은 종류의 폭풍우이다. 그러나 허리케인은 대서양과 태평양 동부에서 형성된다. 그리고 태풍은 태평양 서부에서 형성된다.

허리케인은 미국, 쿠바, 스페인, 브라질과 같은 나라들에 영향을 미친다. 허리케인은 종종 큰 피해를 입힌다. 2005년에 허리케인 카트리나가 미국에 상륙했다. 그것은 뉴올리언스의 도심에 막대한 피해를 입혔다. 그로 인해 2,000여명의 사람들이 죽었다.

아시아에서 태풍은 중국이나 한국, 일본, 필리핀과 같은 나라들에 영향을 미친다. 태풍은 보통 큰 홍수를 일으킨다. 태풍은 또한 많은 사람들을 죽일 수 있다. 2003년에 슈퍼 태풍 매미가 한국을 강타했다. 그 기간 동안 115명의 사람들이 사망했다.

Reading Skills

Atlantic Ocean, Katrina, Pacific Ocean, Maemi

• **Exercise 7** • ──────────────── p.148

정답 Problems: Ⓒ, Ⓔ   Solutions: Ⓑ, Ⓕ

해석 **삼림 벌채 중지**

지구상의 많은 곳에 넓은 삼림 지역이 있다. 그러나 이러한 삼림들이 빠르게 사라지고 있다. 이것은 삼림 벌채 때문이다. 그야말로 사람들이 너무 많은 나무들을 베어내고 있다. 삼림 벌채는 심각한 문제이다. 그러나 그것을 멈출 몇 가지 방법들이 있다.

첫째로, 어떤 국가들은 특정 지역에서 나무를 베는 것을 금하고 있다. 이것은 벌목꾼들이 나무를 벨 수 없다는 것을 의미한다. 이것은 삼림이 다시 자랄 시간을 준다.

또한, 많은 벌목 회사들이 새로운 나무를 심고 있다. 나무는 재생 가능한 자원이다. 그래서 사람들은 나무를 계속해서 사용할 수 있다. 나무를 심음으로써 벌목 회사들은 미래에 더 많은 나무를 벨 수 있을 것이다.

삼림 벌채는 정말 큰 문제이다. 그러나 사람들은 그 일이 일어나지 않도록 막을 방법들을 조금씩 찾고 있다.

Reading Skills

logging, plant

• **Exercise 8** • ──────────────── p.149

정답 Manmade Global Warming: Ⓒ, Ⓕ
Natural Global Warming: Ⓑ, Ⓔ

해석 **지구 온난화**

지구의 기온은 항상 변한다. 어떤 경우에는 매우 춥다. 이러한 시기를 빙하기라고 부른다. 그러나 어떤 경우에는 점점 뜨거워진다. 이러한 시기를 지구 온난화라고 한다. 최근에 지구의 기온이 올라가고 있다. 어떤 사람들은 인류가 이것의 원인이라고 생각한다. 또 다른 사람들은 이것이 자연발생적인 현상이라고 생각한다.

많은 사람들이 인류가 너무 많은 이산화탄소를 만들어 낸다고 생각한다. 이산화탄소는 대기 중으로 올라간다. 그 이산화탄소가 태양열을 가둔다. 그렇게 되면 열은 지구 밖으로 빠져나갈 수 없다. 어떤 사람들에게는 이것이 지구 온난화의 원인이다. 또 다른 사람들은 태양이 점점 뜨거워지고 있다고 생각한다. 그들은 다른 행성들의 온도도 올라가고 있다고 말한다. 그렇기 때문에 지구 온난화가 인류의 산물이 될 수 없다고 말한다. 아무도 진짜 이유를 확실히 알 수 없다. 그러나 과학자들은 지구 온난화를 계속해서 연구할 것이다.

Reading Skills

carbon, sun

Grammar Point   p.150

✓ Grammar Check-Up

Ⓐ 1 ⓒ   2 ⓑ   3 ⓒ   4 ⓐ   5 ⓐ

Ⓑ 1 ⓐ   2 ⓐ   3 ⓒ   4 ⓓ   5 ⓒ

Vocabulary Review   p.152

Ⓐ 1 produces
   2 renewable

3 Deforestation
4 typically
5 traps

B 1 Ⓑ 2 Ⓓ 3 Ⓑ 4 Ⓐ 5 Ⓓ

C 1 Ⓓ 2 Ⓒ 3 Ⓐ 4 Ⓑ 5 Ⓑ

D 1 typhoon
2 clouds
3 planets
4 constantly
5 Countless

Practice Test   p.154

1 Ⓓ 2 Ⓒ 3 Ⓐ 4 Ⓒ 5 ④
6 Oil and gas: ②, ⑥   Renewable Energy: ③, ④, ⑤

해석   재생 가능한 에너지 자원

20세기에 사람들은 많은 새로운 기계들을 사용하기 시작했다. 자동차와 비행기 같은 이러한 기계들은 많은 양의 에너지를 사용한다. 대부분의 경우에 사람들은 기름이나 천연가스로 필요한 에너지를 생산해 냈다. 그러나 오늘날의 많은 과학자들이 전 세계 기름과 가스 매장량이 고갈되고 있다고 믿는다. 그래서 사람들은 다른 종류의 에너지 자원을 찾고 있다. 유망한 에너지 자원으로는 재생 가능한 에너지가 있다.

재생 가능한 에너지는 사람들이 다시 사용할 수 있는 에너지를 말한다. 많은 종류의 재생 가능한 에너지 자원들이 있다. 물은 그중의 하나이다. 많은 댐들이 물을 이용하여 수력 에너지를 만들어낸다. 강물은 끊임없이 흐른다. 그래서 사람들은 그 강물을 사용하여 전기를 계속해서 만들어낼 수 있다.

태양은 또 다른 재생 가능한 에너지이다. 태양 에너지는 사람들이 태양을 이용해 생산하는 에너지이다. 많은 가정에 태양 전지판이 있다. 이러한 판은 태양의 에너지를 모으고 나중에 사용하기 위해 저장한다. 많은 사람들이 태양 에너지를 사용하여 가정에서 물을 데운다. 그러나 태양 에너지를 전적으로 신뢰기는 어렵다. 태양 에너지는 날씨에 좌우된다. 그래서 흐리거나 비가 오는 날에는 사람들이 태양 에너지를 사용하지 못한다. (반면, 날씨가 맑은 날에는 태양 에너지를 매일 사용할 수 있다.)

그 외에도 몇 가지 다른 재생 가능한 에너지 자원들이 있다. 그러나 물과 태양이 가장 일반적인 두 종류이다.

Actual Test

Actual Test 1   p.158

1 Ⓒ 2 Ⓐ 3 Ⓒ 4 Ⓓ 5 Ⓒ 6 Ⓑ
7 Ⓐ 8 Ⓓ 9 ④ 10 ②, ③, ④

해석   미국의 서부 이주

미국이 하나의 국가가 되었을 당시에는 13개의 주가 있었다. 이들은 모두 북아메리카의 동쪽 해안가에 위치해 있었다. 시간이 지나면서 사람들은 서쪽으로 향하기 시작했다. 이러한 서부 이주는 수십 년에 걸쳐 이루어졌다. 하지만 마침내 대서양 해안가부터 태평양 해안까지 사람들이 거주하게 되었다.

1775년에는 약 250만명의 사람들이 미 대륙에 살고 있었다. 이러한 수치는 1700년대 후반과 1800년대에 꾸준히 증가했다. 대부분의 사람들이 유럽에서 건너 왔다. (그들은 새로운 땅에서 새 삶을 시작하기 위해 자신의 고향을 떠났다.) 그들은 본인 소유의 땅을 갖고 싶어 했다. 그 결과 그들은 서쪽으로 이동하기 시작했다.

처음에는 사람들이 오대호 지역 쪽으로 이주를 했다. 이곳은 오늘날의 오하이오, 인디애나, 일리노이, 그리고 미시간 주에 해당하는 땅이었다. 남부 사람들 또한 서쪽으로 이주하기 시작했다. 1800년대에 이르러서는 미시시피강 유역에 많이 정착하였다. 이 강은 북쪽에서 남쪽으로 미국을 남하하며 흘렀다. 하지만 강을 건너는 사람은 거의 없었다.

이러한 상황은 1803년에 바뀌었다. 그해에 토마스 제퍼슨 대통령이 프랑스로부터 루이지애나 영토를 매입했다. 그곳은 미국 크기의 거의 두 배에 이르는 대규모 땅이었다. 점차 꾸준하게, 사람들이 그 땅을 가로질러 서쪽으로 향하기 시작했다. 1800년대 동안 내내 서부 이주가 이루어졌다. 1890년에 이르러서는 미국에 44개의 주가 있었다. 그리고 정부는 서부가 완전히 개척되었다고 선포했다.

Actual Test 2   p.162

1 Ⓒ 2 Ⓑ 3 Ⓐ 4 Ⓒ 5 Ⓑ
6 Ⓓ 7 Ⓓ 8 Ⓑ 9 ②
10 Nature: ①, ③, ⑥   Humans: ②, ⑦

해석   사막화

사막은 지구 표면의 20%를 차지한다. 모든 대륙에 사막이 존재한다. 많은 곳에서 사막이 넓어지고 있다. 이를 사막화라고 부른다. 사막화가 일어나는 데는 많은 원인이 있다. 사막화는 자연과 인간의 활동 때문에 일어날 수 있다.

사막화는 보통 건조 혹은 반건조 지역에서 일어난다. 이 과정에는 몇 가지 단계가 있다. 먼저 많은 수원들이 마르거나 사라진다. 여기에는 지표면 아래의 지하수도 포함된다. 토양의 염도가 높아질 수도 있다. 그로 인해 식물들이 죽기 시작한다. 바람이 비옥한 표토를 날려보내서 식물이 자랄 수 없는 척박한 토양만이 남는 경우도 있다. 이러한 현상들이 모두 새로운 사막을 만들어내는 요인이다.

현재 사막화가 진행되고 있는 곳 중 하나가 사하라 사막이다. 이곳은 북부 아프리카의 거대한 부분을 차지한다. 그 크기 또한 해마다 커지고 있다. 어떤 지역은 1년에 40킬로미터씩 남쪽으로 이동하고 있다. (사하라 사막의 다른 곳에서는 이 현상이 좀 더 느리게 일어나고 있다.) 이곳이 사막이 형성되고 있는 유일한 지역은 아니다. 이러한 일은 아프리카, 오스트레일리아, 아시아, 북아메리카의 다른 지역에서도 일어나고 있다.

대부분의 경우 사막화는 자연적으로 발생한다. 하지만 인간 또한 사막화에 기여할 수 있다. 벌목을 통해 사람들은 토양이 더 쉽게 침식되게 만든다. 그리고 농부들이 지하수를 너무 많이 사용하면 땅이 건조해질 수 있다.

Actual Test 3   p.166

1 Ⓓ 2 Ⓒ 3 Ⓒ 4 Ⓓ 5 Ⓒ 6 Ⓒ
7 Ⓐ 8 Ⓐ 9 ③ 10 ③, ⑤, ⑥

해석 니콜라 테슬라

역사상 가장 뛰어난 발명가 중 한 사람은 니콜라 테슬라였다. 그는 1856년에 태어나 1943년에 사망했다. 그는 여러 다양한 분야를 연구했다. 사망했을 당시 그는 미국에서 100개 이상의 특허권을 보유하고 있었다. 그의 많은 발명들이 중요한 것이었다. 또한 그의 아이디어 중 어떤 것들은 더 많은 현대의 발명들을 이끌었다.

대부분의 사람들이 테슬라를 교류에 대한 그의 연구 때문에 알고 있다. 교류 방식은 전기를 먼 곳까지 효과적으로 내보낸다. 테슬라가 교류를 발명한 것은 아니다. 하지만 그의 연구로 인해 교류가 널리 쓰이게 되었다.

테슬라의 꿈 중 하나는 전선을 사용하지 않고 인류에게 에너지를 공급하는 것이었다. 1891년에 그는 테슬라 코일을 발명했다. 그것은 전선 없이 전기를 전송할 수 있었다. (이것은 오늘날 무선 통신 기술이라고 알려져 있다.) 그것은 처음에 라디오 안테나와 전신에 사용되었다. 또한 이후에는 무선 통신 기술 분야에서 여러 다른 발전들을 이끌어 냈다.

테슬라는 수력 발전 분야에도 기여했다. 그는 나이아가라 폭포에 쓸 발전기를 교류 방식을 이용하여 설계했다. 이는 매우 성공적이었다. 10년 후 미국 전체 전력의 약 10%가 수력 발전으로 생산되었다. 많은 발전소들이 테슬라의 설계를 사용했다.

이들은 그의 발명 중 일부에 불과하다. 심지어 오늘날에도 테슬라의 연구는 전 세계에 엄청난 영향력을 미치고 있다.